Let's EAT MEAT

Let's EAT MEAT

RECIPES FOR
PRIME CUTS,
CHEAP BITS
AND GLORIOUS
SCRAPS OF MEAT
★ ★ ★ ★

TOM PARKER BOWLES

PHOTOGRAPHS BY JENNY ZARINS

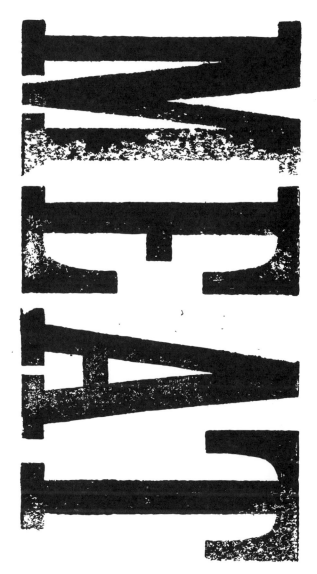

PAVILION

To Mark

First published in the United Kingdom in 2014 by
Pavilion Books Company Limited
1 Gower Street
London WC1E 6HD

ISBN 9781909108318

A CIP catalogue record for this book is available from the British Library.

10 9 8 7 6 5 4 3 2 1

Reproduction by Mission, Hong Kong
Printed and bound by 1010 Printing International Limited, China

This book can be ordered direct from the publisher at
www.pavilionbooks.com

Commissioning editor: Becca Spry
Designer: Miranda Harvey
Art editor: Laura Russell
Photographer: Jenny Zarins
Food stylist: Justine Pattison
Stylists: Pene Parker and Sarah O'Keefe
Illustrations: Matthew Allen
Copy editor: Maggie Ramsay

CONTENTS

INTRODUCTION

This is a book about meat. No surprises there. The title rather gives it away. But rather than batter you about the head with a frozen leg of lamb while ordering you to feast on more flesh, I'm proposing we should eat less.

If there is anything as lofty as a philosophy coursing through this book, it's this: eat meat, but eat less, and eat better. I'm not saying we should stint on great hunks of beef, carved tissue-paper thin and drowned in torrents of glistening gravy. Nor forgo thick, charred steaks (*see* page 16) or golden-crusted deep-fried chicken (*see* page 63). There are recipes for these classics in the book, along with slow-cooked lamb (*see* page 46), Chinese roast duck (*see* page 67), Goan pork curry (*see* page 34), a rich jambalaya (*see* page 36), and stews from France (*see* page 55) and Indonesia (*see* page 22). These are not so much everyday dishes, but feasts to relish. It's these recipes that make up the bulk of the first chapter, *Meat*.

In the *Less Meat* chapter, things get, well, a little less carnivorous. Meat still plays a role in the recipes, but is no longer the star. It shares the spotlight with potatoes, rice, pasta or pastry. Hardly the most arduous of tasks, I know. From a mighty Britalian lasagne (*see* page 74) and typically Roman spaghetti all'amatriciana (*see* page 87) to bun cha – Vietnamese pork and noodles (*see* page 79). Or a sturdy Iberian bean stew, perked up with a few chunks of frazzled, fat-flecked chorizo (*see* page 93). Even salads that introduce crisp duck to cool watermelon (*see* page 115) or green leaves and croutons (*see* page 112).

And then there's *Meat as Seasoning*, a chapter devoted to little blasts of flavour that a pork bone can give to a broth or a few shreds of bacon to a bowlful of beans. The flavours still zip across the tongue, hot, salty, sour or sweet, but the meat is happy, indeed demands, to take more of a backseat role. A cameo, if you will, but one essential to the final plot. Marlon Brando in *Superman*, Judi Dench in *Shakespeare in Love*. Think of America's Deep South, with its black-eyed peas (*see* page 125), Scotland's stovies, potato cakes flavoured with a little beef shin (*see* page 120), Sichuan green beans (*see* page 123) with pork mince, and endless ways with preserved pig. Necessity is the mother of invention and all that.

Not forgetting game and offal, that woefully under-rated pair of flavour saviours. Braised ox cheek pie (*see* page 166), kidneys in sherry (*see* page 168), and neat piles of the softest venison tartare (*see* page 174). Nothing to fear, everything to embrace.

There's even a chapter called *No Meat*. This isn't some half-hearted, tacked-on and entirely spurious section at the back, rather an integral part of the book. These are dishes to eat alongside meat or even, dare I say it, by themselves. Good food is about flavour, and I'm equally happy eating beautifully spiced aloo dum as I am attacking a rib of beef.

Because in the rich, well-padded Western world, we eat too much meat. Way, way too much. The vast majority is from chickens. And most are not the happily scratching, born-free Chicken Lickens that peck and cluck around the farmyard floor, scratching for grubs and awaiting the imminent implosion of the sky. No, these are wretched, much-abused beasts, animals as mere financial unit. Even the most callous and blood-stained of carnivores might struggle to support a system of farming where the chickens' legs buckle under the weight of their grotesquely (and unnaturally) inflated breasts. We like breasts, you see, caring little that they usually taste of the square root of bugger all.

Intensively farmed birds are bred for quick profit, rather than deep flavour, and to aid this unnatural process, the birds are routinely dosed with antibiotics. This not only produces unhappy, inferior-tasting birds, but when passed on to us through the food chain, actually stops prescribed drugs doing what they should. Already there are certain strains of bacteria against which conventional antibiotics have no hope. Scary stuff.

The intensively farmed pigs get an equally abhorrent deal. Because, unluckily for them, these highly intelligent beasts respond well to all manner of strange scientific tinkering. Their diet is cheap and high in protein (to make them grow to weight more rapidly) and they often end their short, miserable lives in vast slaughterhouses that don't manage to kill them properly, often just leaving them stunned before they're fed into artificial infernos, meant to singe off the bristles. The world of intensive farming is as myopic as it is cruel. Everyone's a loser in the constant quest for cheap meat. And its long-term costs are immense: to the animals' welfare, to our planet and to our health.

As Alex Renton writes in his excellent *Planet Carnivore*, 'cheap meat means corners cut on safety, health and welfare: humane treatment generally slows down the production line.' Which is why good, ethically produced meat is more expensive. To allow a pig, chicken, cow or sheep to grow naturally costs more money. As does a varied, high-quality feed.

Intensive farming is responsible for wildlife decimation, as natural habitats are ripped up, soils rendered arid and infertile by the constant flood of herbicides and pesticides. In America, it's got to the point where bees have to be trucked in to pollinate the Californian almond blossom. The chemicals used in the mass production of these nuts have simply obliterated the native swarm. These sort of facts chill me to the bone. In Philip Lymbery's *Farmageddon: The True Cost of Cheap Meat*, he travels the globe, reporting on the nicotine-stained smogs that lurk above the super-dairies, and the river of effluent that leaches into the water table, river and sea, a by-product of the vast, unthinking farming of chickens and pigs and cows on a near super-human scale. Now I'm no hippy. But really, this has gone too far. It's down to us to act.

You only have to look at the horsemeat scandal of 2013 to find out how little most of us know about the meat we're eating. I have no problem with a good horse tartare. But if I order beef, I do like to know it comes from a mooer, rather than a neigher. And if you're getting a frozen burger for about five pence, you can be fairly sure there's a lot of cheap filler in there. And perhaps a soupçon of Shergar.

But what about the folk who can't afford to drop £10 on a decent chicken? Good-quality meat, they argue, is a rich man's treat, for the smug, Prius-driving, Ocado-shopping, middle-class elite. But do we really need to eat meat every day? By giving it a rest sometimes, you'll have more cash to spend on the good stuff. And if you do buy a decent chicken, not only will your taste buds rejoice, but you will get three meals rather than one. The roast chicken, chicken sandwiches the next day and, every bit as thrilling, proper stock made from the bones. It's plain culinary common sense.

I may still be many hundreds of miles removed from being a full-time vegetarian. But the older I get, the more joy I find in legumes and sheer delight in every form of vegetable, be it green and leafy or a root, covered in soil. The idea of a meat-free Monday or Tuesday or whenever is simple: don't stop eating meat, rather have one day a week without it. It's sensible and pragmatic, and really what this book is about.

One last word. Do trust your butcher. Find a good one, and, in the words of the Blues Brothers, 'When you do find that somebody. Hold that woman, hold that man.' Well, you know what I mean. Don't be misled or dazzled by labels, rare breeds, organic this, or biodynamic that. Just taste it. The vast majority of meat that has a decent flavour will have been brought up by a farmer who cares about proper farming practice. It's as simple as that. Any butcher worth his well-hung forerib will be only too thrilled to tell you about how long the beef has been hung, or from which breed it comes. He'll also give you advice on how to cook the more unusual cuts.

Meat is not a necessity. We don't need it to survive, but when properly produced, it becomes one of life's greatest joys. I have no intention of eschewing pork or beef or lamb or chicken. I just want less, and better. It's that simple. And everyone's a winner. Your purse, your health, your conscience, your country and your palate. Oh, and not forgetting the animals, too. But the lecture's over. I'm getting hungry. It's time for lunch.

This chapter, as you might guess, is the one where a great hunk of flesh is the star and main event. A whole bird, a hulking shoulder, a mighty rib. The sort of joint that could open a Hollywood blockbuster, or have its own range of scent. I make no apologies. This is the *Meat* part of the book, blatantly flesh-obsessed, filled with recipes from the US and Mexico, Japan and Britain, Italy, France, Spain, Portugal, India and China, and best saved for long, languorous lunches that stretch merrily into dinner. Or riotous feasts that carouse on for days. Meat as celebration, as the centrepiece. *Let's Eat Meat* indeed.

When choosing meat, remember that unhappy beasts rarely make good eating. I don't mean that a manic-depressive Gloucester Old Spot is unsuited to the spit, nor a melancholic Manx lamb unfit for the oven. Rather, an animal that is allowed space to rootle, wander and peck, given a good, varied diet and time to grow as nature intended, will invariably taste better than some intensively reared wretch. It's a basic principle, and one unclouded by either sanctimonious finger-wagging, or the sickly witterings of dewy-eyed anthropomorphism.

In a book dedicated to eating less meat, but better, quality is everything. For those of you lucky enough to be on first-name terms with your local butcher, take a bow. A good butcher is the swiftest and easiest way to good-quality, naturally reared meat. But for those of you not blessed with a moustachioed master with tattooed forearms like great prize gammons, meat-buying can be a bore. We're bombarded with labels and 'buzz words'. 'Free-range', 'organic', 'rare-breed', 'dry-aged', and God knows what else. All of these can produce wonderful meat, and all can produce second-rate pap. Labels alone are simply no indicator of fundamental quality. Your taste buds, on the other hand, are a whole lot more revealing.

Take rare-breed beef. 'The Belted Galloway', some might say, 'is the greatest-tasting breed of them all.' Others disagree, arguing for the merits of Longhorn over White Park, or the bovine heft of the Aberdeen Angus over Hereford. Although the popularity of traditional breeds is stirring stuff, when it comes to eating, breed is one part of a complex jigsaw.

You might have the most glorious-looking Belted Galloway mooer, but unless you know how to feed it properly (mainly outdoor grass, for example, rather than cheaper barley, which has a higher protein content, meaning the cow grows faster and costs less to produce); finish it well (a crucial stage in the last six months of the animal's life, when the protein in the feed is increased to create a good hard layer of fat); slaughter humanely, with minimum stress; hang (an essential process that intensifies flavour and tenderises flesh); and expertly butcher it, the noble lineage comes to nought. The art of raising great meat, be it cow, sheep, chicken or pig, is about farmers who not only know what they're doing, but farm for flavour over a swift, easy buck.

Rare-breed beasts can be a splendid thing. Be it Southdown lamb ('the best in England', according to the great Dorothy Hartley) or Tamworth, Essex or Berkshire pig. But as ever in matters of taste, try to ignore the labels, and answer the one question that matters: What does the thing taste like? If it thrills the palate, you can be pretty sure the farmer not only knew what he was doing, but treated the animal in a humane way. Good meat doesn't come from rare breeds, rather from good farming practice.

Steak grilled over mesquite wood (or briquettes, or plain charcoal), sliced very thinly, then wrapped in soft corn tortillas with grilled spring onions, salsa, a dollop of guacamole, a dash of hot sauce, pickled onions and raw shredded cabbage. It's not so much a dish as a generic term, also called carne asada. *You'll find variations from Texas right down to Oaxaca. The smell is intoxicating. It's best cooked over coals, but can be done in a griddle pan.*

Tacos al Carbon

SERVES 4

2 large sirloin or skirt steaks
   (about 300g/10½oz each)
groundnut or sunflower oil
sea salt and freshly ground
   black pepper
12 spring onions
12 corn tortillas
hot sauce, such as Tabasco
¼ small cabbage, shredded
lime wedges, for squeezing

PICKLED RED ONION
½ red onion, thinly sliced
½ habanero chilli, thinly sliced
1 tbsp white wine vinegar

PICO DE GALLO
2 tomatoes, peeled, deseeded
   and roughly chopped
2 long green finger chillies,
   deseeded and finely chopped
½ small onion, roughly
   chopped
juice of ½ lime
handful of coriander leaves,
   roughly chopped

GUACAMOLE
3 avocados
1 red onions, finely chopped
1 jalapeño or finger chillies,
   finely chopped
2 tomatoes, peeled, deseeded
   and finely chopped
juice of 1 lime

Light your barbecue and wait until the coals are white-hot, or heat your griddle pan until it's smoking hot. Brush the steaks with oil, season well with salt, then grill for 2 minutes on each side. Leave to rest for 2 minutes. This will give rare steak. Slice very thinly.

Brush the spring onions with oil, season and cook for 4–6 minutes, until charred. Cut them in half, slice into 2cm/¾-inch pieces, or leave whole.

Heat the tortillas on the barbecue (or in a hot dry pan), then wrap them in a tea cloth to keep warm. Serve the steak on one plate, the tortillas on another, and the spring onions, pickled red onion, pico de gallo, guacamole, cabbage and lime wedges in small bowls alongside and put the Tabasco on the table. Let people pimp their tacos however they wish.

Pickled Red Onion

Put the onion and habanero chilli in a small bowl with the vinegar, cover and marinate for 1 hour. Drain and serve.

Pico de Gallo

Mix the tomatoes, green chillies, onion and lime juice in a bowl. Add salt to taste and leave for 1 hour. Stir in the coriander, then serve.

Guacamole

Peel, stone and mash the avocados roughly using a large fork. Add the red onions, jalapeño chillies, tomatoes and lime juice. Season to taste and serve.

We don't hear much about Indonesian food, but as Jill Norman – that great editor and writer – once told me, the British simply don't have a taste for it. But, as dusk falls over Bali and Lombok, a thousand small charcoal stoves light up, grilling pieces of pork (in Bali, a mainly Hindu country) and water buffalo or beef. I adapted this recipe from Indonesian Regional Food and Cookery, *a true classic by Sri Owen, one of my heroes and the great expert on all things edible and Asian. If you don't like chilli heat, omit the* sambal ulek. *But you do need to use minced steak, rather than cheap mince.*

Indonesian Minced Beef Satay

SERVES 4

600g/1lb 5oz rump steak,
   minced
pinch of sea salt
juice of 1 lime
vegetable oil for brushing

SPICE PASTE
2 tsp coriander seeds, toasted
2 shallots, roughly chopped
2 garlic cloves, roughly
   chopped
1.5cm/½-inch piece of fresh
   ginger, peeled and roughly
   chopped
big pinch of soft brown sugar
1 tbsp light soy sauce
2 tsp sambal ulek (optional, *see*
   page 218)

Mix the mince with the salt and lime juice and set aside.

To make the spice paste, put the coriander seeds in a mortar and pestle and bash until finely ground. Tip into a small blender, then add the remaining ingredients and blitz to a paste.

Mix the spice paste thoroughly with the meat, then, if possible, cover and leave in the fridge to firm up for a couple of hours. Shape into walnut-sized ovals.

Soak 12 wooden skewers in water for at least 30 minutes (alternatively, use metal skewers). Light your barbecue and wait until the coals are white-hot, or heat your griddle pan until it's smoking hot.

Put four beef balls onto each skewer and grill for about 4 minutes, turning every now and then. Brush with oil and cook for a further 2 minutes, or until cooked. Serve hot.

This comes in at the more exotic end of the Thai curry spectrum; when done in a truly authentic way it takes much time and effort. But what's wrong with time and effort when the result is this magnificent? It's more spice-warm than chilli-hot, and it's said it arrived from Persia some time in the sixteenth century. Although, as is ever the case with much-loved regional dishes, it is also claimed to have come from southern Thailand, where there are plenty of Muslims, who arrived with Indian or Arab traders. Toasting the spices first helps bring out their essential oils.

Mussaman Beef Curry

To make the spice paste, put the chillies and salt in a large mortar and pestle and grind, then slowly bash in the rest of the ingredients. Or throw everything in a small blender and blitz to a thickish paste, adding a little water if necessary. Set aside.

Heat the oil in a large, heavy-bottomed pot and cook the spice paste over a low heat until fragrant. Do not burn.

Add the steak chunks and cook until just browned. Add the coconut cream and milk, sugar, ginger, fish sauce, cinnamon stick and half the tamarind water and stir. Cook for a couple of minutes, then cover and simmer gently for 2 hours, adding a little water if the sauce begins to stick. (Alternatively, cover and cook in a preheated oven at fan 150°C/300°F/Gas 3 for 1½–2 hours, until the beef is tender and the sauce is thick and glossy.)

Stir in the remaining tamarind water and serve with rice.

Tamarind water

Put a 25g/1oz chunk of dried tamarind in a bowl, cover with 150ml/5fl oz just-boiled water and leave for 10 minutes. Press through a sieve into another bowl. Transfer the pressed tamarind back to the first bowl and cover with another 150ml/5fl oz just-boiled water. Leave for 10 minutes and press through the sieve again. (Alternatively, mix 2 tsp tamarind paste with 100ml/3½fl oz cold water.)

SERVES 4

2 tbsp groundnut oil

400g/14oz braising steak, cut into 3cm/1¼-inch chunks

200g/7oz solid creamed coconut

400ml/14fl oz can of unsweetened coconut milk

3 tbsp palm (or caster) sugar

7cm/3-inch piece of fresh ginger, peeled, finely grated

2 tbsp fish sauce

½ cinnamon stick

5 tbsp tamarind water (see method)

steamed jasmine rice, to serve

SPICE PASTE

7–15 dried red chillies, deseeded and white part scraped away, soaked in just-boiled water for 20 minutes, drained

big pinch of sea salt

100g/3½oz chunk of fresh coconut, finely grated

4 garlic cloves, roughly chopped

2 tsp cumin seeds, toasted

2 tbsp unsalted peanuts, toasted

2 bay leaves

5 cloves, toasted

1 lemongrass stalk, chopped

OK, so we all know this was created in Harry's Bar in Venice, for a picky aristo who had been told by her doctor/quack to eat raw beef. The bar's owner, Giuseppe Cipriani, a highly enterprising sort, took inspiration from the posters advertising an exhibition of Vittore Carpaccio (a painter who loved his red and white), and came up with a dish of thinly sliced fillet drizzled with olive oil, lemon and Parmesan. This is a variation on the classic. I add horseradish for a bit more oomph. Fillet works well, as does sirloin. Briefly freezing the meat makes it easier to slice. As ever with raw meat, make sure the quality is flawless.

Beef Carpaccio my way

Put the beef on a piece of clingflim, wrap very tightly and secure at each end, making a beefy sausage. Freeze overnight.

To make the horseradish sauce, mix all the ingredients together, adding more crème fraîche if you want to tone down that oomph. Or less if you really want to blast your nostrils. Set aside.

Take the beef out of the freezer and leave to stand for 15 minutes. Carve it into slices as thinly as you can. A slicer is ideal, but not essential.

Spread the beef over four plates, almost covering them, then season with salt, pepper and a glug of olive oil.

Serve the carpaccio with a few blobs of horseradish sauce.

SERVES 4

600g/1lb 5oz beef fillet, trimmed of excess fat
sea salt and freshly ground black pepper
good glug of extra virgin olive oil

HORSERADISH SAUCE
chunk of fresh horseradish, the size of a man's index finger (about 20g/¾oz), peeled and finely grated
about 5 tbsp crème fraîche
1 tsp white wine vinegar

Indonesia's food gets something of a bum deal in the wider world. The vast and sprawling archipelago has all manner of searing sambals and satays, as well as endless wonderful ways with pig and chicken. And what is it famous for? A pile of rice topped with a fried egg, aka nasi goreng, *that gap-year student favourite. But the more I find out about Indonesian food, the more I wonder why we don't embrace it. Beef rendang is a star dish, beef slow cooked in spiced coconut milk, and 'the one dish', according to the food writer Sri Owen, that 'passes from boiling to frying in a continuous process'. It was originally used to slightly preserve fresh buffalo. The process would tenderise the meat and prolong its life, as well as giving it a wonderful taste. It should be rich and rather exotic, the beef falling apart at the mere mention of fork.*

Beef Rendang

SERVES 4–5

1 tbsp vegetable or groundnut
  oil
1kg/2lb 4oz beef shin, cut into
  4–5cm/1½–2-inch chunks
2 lemongrass stalks, trimmed
1 cinnamon stick
2 x 400ml/14fl oz cans of
  unsweetened coconut milk
2 bay leaves
big pinch of sea salt
steamed sticky rice, to serve

SPICE PASTE

4 cloves
½ whole nutmeg, grated
6–10 fresh red chillies,
  roughly chopped
6 shallots, peeled
4 garlic cloves, peeled
1 tsp ground turmeric
5cm/2-inch piece of fresh
  ginger, peeled
5cm/2-inch piece of fresh
  galangal, peeled, or ½ tsp
  galangal powder

To make the spice paste, put the cloves and nutmeg in a small blender and grind. Add the rest of the ingredients and blitz to a thick paste.

Heat the oil in a large, heavy-bottomed pan, then add the paste and cook over a medium heat until fragrant. Add the beef, increase the heat to high and mix well, so the meat is well coated in the spices.

Put the lemongrass on a board and bash once or twice with the thick side of a knife. Add it to the pan with the cinnamon stick, coconut milk and bay leaves. Reduce the heat to medium, cover the pan loosely with a lid and simmer for about 3 hours, stirring often and adding about 150ml/5fl oz of water every now and then if the sauce looks very thick, until the beef is coated in a rich, dark sauce.

Remove the lemongrass, cinnamon stick and bay leaves, season with salt, then serve with the sticky rice.

There are a shed load of peppercorns in this stew — enough to clear even Jupiter's nostrils. You might expect a recipe like this to come from ancient Siam, and be made with buffalo. After all, pepper was used for pungency before chilli arrived with the Portuguese in the early sixteenth century. But no, this comes from Tuscany, a part of Italy not exactly known for its spice. Apparently it was once cooked in the Florentine kilns that made the terracotta tiles for the Duomo. And it was a peasant dish. This romantic tale might have an element of truth, but it would be a mighty rich bunch of peasants who could afford this much beef and pepper. Originally it would have been made without tomatoes. This dish is nowhere near as fierce as you'd expect. Think generous warmth rather than nose-blasting bite.

Peposo

SERVES 4

**1kg/2lb 4oz stewing beef, such
  as shin, shank or cheek, cut
  into large pieces (roughly
  the size of a child's fist)**
**sea salt and freshly ground
  black pepper**
4 tbsp olive oil
6 garlic cloves, chopped
1 onion, chopped
1 bay leaf
**20g/¾oz whole black
  peppercorns**
**a good grinding of black
  pepper**
**75cl bottle of red wine
  (Chianti would be perfect)**
**2 x 400g/14oz cans of
  chopped tomatoes**
1 tsp caster sugar (optional)
good bread, to serve

Preheat the oven to fan 150°C/300°F/Gas 3. Season the meat with salt. Heat half the oil in a heavy ovenproof dish over a medium–high heat and brown the meat in batches, adding more oil if needed. The meat should acquire a proper dark tan, rather than an anaemic grey tinge. Using a slotted spoon, transfer it to a large plate and set aside.

Add a little more oil to the pan, add the garlic and onion and cook for about 10 minutes, until soft. Then put the meat back in the pan. Add the bay leaf, peppercorns and enough ground black pepper to blacken the meat, and cook for a minute or so.

Add the wine, tomatoes and sugar, if using, and bring to a simmer. Cover the pan and bake for 3–4 hours, until very tender. Serve with good bread.

WHY WE ROCK at

ROASTING

'Oh! The Roast Beef of England, And old English Roast Beef.' Henry Fielding, progenitor of the novel and scribe of lascivious good times, certainly knew his grub. And in his lusty love letter to roast beef and patriotism, part of *The Grub Street Opera*, roast beef plays a starring role. 'When mighty Roast Beef was the Englishman's food,' cries the ballad, 'It ennobled our brains and enriched our blood.' This is Rule Britannia on a plate, served bloody with a fierce, flag-waving pile of mustard alongside.

'Our soldiers were brave and our courtiers were good,' *The Grub Street Opera* goes on, looking wistfully back to an imagined golden age, intoxicated by the fervour of its native adoration. And it gets in the requisite swipe about those cheese-eating, garlic-munching popinjays across La Manche. 'But since we have learnt from all-vapouring France; To eat their ragouts as well as to dance; We're fed up with nothing but vain complaisance.' Quite.

Henri Misson was a rare Frenchman who loved English food. *Quelle horreur!* Travelling through the land towards the end of the seventeenth century, he describes the cook houses, with 'Generally, four spits, one over another, carry round each five or six pieces of butcher's meat, beef, mutton, veal, pork and lamb; you have what quantity you please cut off, fat, lean, much or little done; with this, a little salt and mustard upon the side of your plate, a bottle of beer and a roll; and there is your whole feast.' He also extols the quality of our cows. Per Kalm was another foreign enthusiast, writing in the eighteenth century: 'Roast meat is the Englishman's delice and principal dish. The English roasts are remarkable for two things. 1) All English meat... has a fatness and delicious taste; 2) The Englishmen understand almost better than any other people the art of properly roasting a joint.'

OK, so the French took gastronomy to a higher art than we did. But why is it that we were, and still are, masters of roasting? We certainly had lots of wood. A basic but fundamental requirement. Mesolithic Britons had neither pottery nor metal kits to cook their food, so roasting was the simplest and most effective way of cooking, turned on a green forest spit. Food was either cooked 'warm' from the kill, as was popular among various hirsute Goths of the first century, or hung, to tenderise it. Celts were roasters too (although they also stewed).

'The "taste of the fire" was what the Englishman liked,' writes Elisabeth Ayrton in *The Cookery of England*. Robert May, in *The Accomplisht Cook* (1660), lists seven dredgings ('to prevent the gravy from too much evaporating'), from flour mixed with bread to fennel seeds, coriander, cinnamon and sugar. And basting, using everything from butter and suet to egg yolks and orange juice. A high art indeed. But as the nineteenth century dawned, so stoves and ranges appeared, and spits died out. Something which, according to Rupert Croft-Cooke in *English Cooking*, saw 'the last decline of English cooking', from 'the time when we ceased to roast our meat and started to bake it in the oven'.

I'm not sure I agree. Although meat licked by flame is magnificent. Home roasting wasn't common until about a century back. Fuel was expensive, so most people would use the local baker's oven, or buy meat ready roasted from the taverns and chophouses that abounded in big cities. But quality is everything. With roasting there's nowhere to hide, no sauce to cover up any imperfections. Start with a fine bit of meat. The rest is simply a matter of practice.

This is all about the beef, and doing as little as possible to it. I find a three- or four-rib roast will happily serve six, with lots of leftovers for sandwiches and the rest. I like mine very rare, but still a little warm in the middle.

Roast Rib of Beef

SERVES 6

3–4 bone rib of beef
2–3 tbsp olive oil
1 tbsp Worcestershire sauce
1 tbsp English mustard
 powder
sea salt and freshly ground
 black pepper

Preheat the oven to fan 220°C/425°F/Gas 9. Weigh the beef and make a note of the weight.

Rub the oil all over the beef, then douse it with Worcestershire sauce and sprinkle over the mustard. Season heartily, then put it in a roasting tin and bang it into the oven.

Roast for 20 minutes, turn the oven down to fan 170°C/340°F/Gas 5 and roast for another 10 minutes per 250g.

Leave to rest in a warm place for 20 minutes before carving.

Less a slow-cooked American stew, more an edible Southern historical fracas. For years, Brunswick County, North Carolina, has claimed this dish as its own. As have the good folk of Brunswick town, Georgia. The people of Brunswick County Virginia have a strong historical claim too; something about Dr Creed Haskins, a politician, who wanted to cook something memorable for a political rally. As to what makes it 'authentic' … there have been versions made with pork, beef, turkey, rabbit, squirrel, lamb, goat and possum. Apparently, it must contain at least two meats. As well as beans, okra, corn, tomatoes, potatoes and other veg. And that's just the start. Arguments rage over cooking time, texture, colour and whether it's best eaten with hush puppies (deep-fried cornmeal batter), cornbread or biscuits, remembering that in North America, a 'biscuit' is what Brits call a scone. My advice: keep out of the battle. It's wonderful, best made in big batches. Eat up, y'all.

Brunswick Stew

Preheat the oven to fan 200°C/400°F/Gas 7. Roast the bones on a baking tray for 30 minutes.

Heat the oil in a huge stockpot and brown the chicken all over; set aside. Then brown the ham hock and set aside.

In the same pot, cook the onions, celery, carrot and chilli until the vegetables are soft, then put the chicken and ham hock back into the pan, along with the Worcestershire sauce, paprika and the roasted bones. Add cold water to cover by about 2.5cm/1 inch (about 8 litres/14 pints), bring to the boil and then skim.

Simmer for 3 hours, then remove the chicken, ham and bones. Shred the chicken and ham, discarding the skin and bones.

Pass the stock through a sieve into another large pan and skim excess fat from the top. Bring to the boil and reduce until you have around 3 litres/5¼ pints of liquid; this will take around 30 minutes.

Return the meat to the pot, add the beans, sweetcorn and tomatoes and cook for 15 minutes, stirring occasionally.

Add the potatoes and cook for 15 minutes, until the potatoes are tender and the stew is properly thick. Season to taste. Serve with bread (traditionally cornbread, hush puppies or biscuits).

SERVES 10–12

1kg/2lb 4oz beef or veal shin bones
3 tbsp sunflower oil
1 large (2kg/4lb 8oz) chicken
1 uncooked ham hock
3 onions, roughly chopped
3 celery stalks, roughly chopped
1 large carrot, roughly chopped
2 big pinches of dried chilli flakes
2 tbsp Worcestershire sauce
1 tsp paprika
250g/9oz butter beans, soaked in cold water overnight, or 2 x 400g/14oz cans of butter beans, drained
900g/2lb raw sweetcorn kernels, or 2 x 326g/11½oz cans of sweetcorn, drained
2 x 400g/14oz cans of chopped tomatoes
500g/1lb 2oz floury potatoes, peeled and cut into thick slices
sea salt and freshly ground pepper
bread, to serve

Damn, I love this dish, soft slices of beef lurking in an oily, chilli bath thick with numbing Sichuan pepper and dried Sichuan chillies. Just as important, when I order it at Pearl Liang in Paddington, west London, everyone takes one look and grimaces at the amount of chillies and the slick torrent of oil, leaving it all to me. The chillies are hot but not searing and the whole dish is quietly strident, a riot of fine tastes and textures. And rather than try to replicate the recipe myself, I've turned to Fuchsia Dunlop, expert in all things Sichuan and author of the brilliant Sichuan Cookery.

Sichuan Boiled Beef

SERVES 4

500g/1lb 2oz sirloin steak, trimmed of excess fat

sea salt

1 tbsp Shaoxing rice wine, mirin or medium-dry sherry

1 head of celery

4 spring onions

8–10 dried red chillies

150ml/5fl oz groundnut oil

2 tsp Sichuan pepper

4 tbsp potato flour or cornflour, mixed with 4 tbsp cold water

3 tbsp chilli bean paste (or chilli bean sauce)

700ml/1¼ pints chicken stock (cube is fine)

2 tsp dark soy sauce

Cut the beef against the grain into thin slices about 2.5 x 5cm/ 1 x 2 inches. Add ¼ tsp salt and the wine, mix well, then cover and leave to marinate in the fridge while you prepare everything else.

Remove the fibrous outer edge of the celery. Chop each stalk into three or four pieces, then slice these lengthwise into 1cm/½-inch wide sticks. Gently crush the spring onions and chop them into 3 pieces to match the celery. Wearing rubber gloves, snip the chillies in half, discarding as many seeds as possible.

Heat 3 tbsp oil in a wok until hot but not quite smoking. Add the chillies and Sichuan pepper and stir-fry until they are fragrant and the chillies are just beginning to brown (take care not to burn them). Immediately slide the spices into a bowl, leaving the oil in the wok. When the chillies have cooled down a little, transfer them to a chopping board and chop them finely with a gentle rocking motion, using a cleaver taken in both hands or a two-handled chopper. Set them aside.

Return the oily wok to the stove over a high heat. When it is smoking, add the celery and spring onions and stir-fry for 1–2 minutes, adding ¼–½ tsp salt to taste, until they are hot and just-cooked but still crunchy. Tip them into a serving bowl.

Add the potato flour mixture to the beef and stir well in one direction to coat all the meat. Heat another 3 tbsp oil in the wok over a high heat, until just beginning to smoke. Turn the heat down to medium, add the chilli bean paste, and stir-fry for about 30 seconds, until the oil is red and fragrant. Add the

stock and soy sauce, season with salt to taste, and return to the boil over a high heat. When the sauce is boiling vigorously, drop in the beef and potato starch mixture. Wait for the sauce to return to the boil, then use a pair of chopsticks to gently separate the slices. Simmer for a minute or so, until the beef is just cooked, and then spoon it onto the waiting vegetables. Pour over the sauce.

Rinse out the wok and dry it well. Heat another 3–4 tbsp of oil in the wok until smoking. Sprinkle the chopped chillies and Sichuan pepper over the beef dish, then pour over the smoking oil, which will sizzle dramatically. If you move quickly, the dish will still be fizzing when you bring it to the table.

When I see this breadcrumb-clad beauty on the menu, little else matters. I couldn't care less if it's retro, or in or out of fashion. It's a northern European classic, simply schnitzel with added punch – topped with a fried egg, capers and anchovies. The Wolseley in London does a wonderful version, but I wish they wouldn't add the gravy. As for the veal, try to go for British rose veal. It doesn't have quite the same bland tenderness as the Continental milk-fed veal (in fact, it's almost a different product entirely), but as the calves are allowed space to move around and have a more natural, mixed diet, you can eat with conscience clear.

Veal Holstein

SERVES 4

25g/1oz plain flour
big pinch of mustard powder
sea salt and freshly ground
    black pepper
6 large eggs
100g/3½oz fresh breadcrumbs
4 veal escalopes (about
    150g/5½oz each), bashed
    between two pieces of
    clingfilm with a rolling pin
    until almost paper-thin
150g/5½oz unsalted butter
1 tbsp sunflower oil
2 heaped tbsp non-pareil
    capers, drained
2 tbsp finely chopped fresh
    parsley
juice of ½ lemon
8 anchovy fillets (the best you
    can find), drained

Season the flour with the mustard powder, salt and pepper, and put it on a plate. Break two of the eggs into a shallow bowl and beat lightly. Put the breadcrumbs in a bowl. Lightly season the veal, dip in the seasoned flour, then the beaten egg, then the breadcrumbs.

Melt 50g/1¾oz butter with the oil in a large, heavy-bottomed frying pan over a medium heat and cook the escalopes, two at a time, until golden – about 1½–2 minutes on each side. Remove and keep warm.

Wipe out the pan with a wad of kitchen paper, add half the remaining butter and fry the eggs. Top each escalope with a runny-yolked fried egg.

Melt the remaining butter in the pan, add the capers and warm for a few seconds, then remove from the heat and add the parsley and a good squeeze of lemon.

Criss-cross each egg with two anchovy fillets, spoon over the capers and parsley and serve with French fries or sautéed potatoes.

There's nothing wrong with the post-pub vindaloo, the chilli-powder-laced bruiser that brawls its way through the digestive system with little regard for civilised calm. It does have its own crude, rough-hewn charms. The real thing, though, is rather different, a handsome, worldly charmer, with Portuguese roots, and lashings of pork, vinegar and chilli. There's a more complex recipe in my previous book, Let's Eat, *but this version manages to contain the soul of vindaloo, without quite as much of the hassle — as long as you remember to marinate the meat a day ahead.*

Old-Fashioned Goan Vindaloo

SERVES 4

800g/1lb 12oz leg of pork, trimmed of excess fat and cut into 4cm/1½-inch chunks

3–4 tbsp vegetable oil

1½ tbsp black peppercorns, roughly crushed

½ cinnamon stick

4–8 long green finger chillies, halved

3 onions, finely chopped

1 tsp Demerara sugar (or jaggery if you can get it)

1 tsp sea salt flakes, or to taste

handful of fresh coriander leaves, roughly chopped

boiled basmati rice, to serve

SPICE PASTE

10–15 dried Kashmiri chillies (or long red Indian chillies), soaked in just-boiled water for 20 minutes, drained

6 garlic cloves

2.5cm/1-inch piece of fresh ginger, peeled

1 tsp cumin seeds, toasted until fragrant, then ground in a mortar and pestle

7–8 tbsp malt vinegar (or coconut vinegar)

To make the spice paste, in a small blender, blitz the drained chillies with the garlic, ginger, cumin and 6 tbsp of the vinegar. Mix the paste thoroughly with the pork, cover and marinate in the fridge overnight.

The next day, heat 3 tbsp oil in a large pan and add the peppercorns, cinnamon and fresh chillies and cook gently for a couple of minutes. Turn up the heat, add the pork and cook until it has a good brown crust all over, adding a little extra oil if necessary. Remove the meat and transfer it to a plate. Add the onions and cook over a medium–low heat for about 15 minutes, until soft and golden.

Add the sugar and about 250ml/9fl oz water, plus a splash of vinegar. Bring to a low simmer, cover and cook for 1 hour. Add about 200ml/7fl oz water to prevent sticking. Remove the lid and cook for a further 1½ hours, adding more water if necessary, until the meat falls apart. Stir in an extra tbsp of vinegar and salt to taste, sprinkle with coriander and serve with basmati rice.

This recipe was inspired by a night out in Tokyo. The details are sketchy, seeing as I'd spent the previous few hours murdering the back catalogue of The Rolling Stones while inhaling stupid amounts of whisky. But we ended up in some backstreet, where the air was thick with the scent of grilling bird and beast and I was faced with entire battalions of yakitori, using every part of the chicken from breast to cartilage and guts. All very good. But it was the skewers of pork belly that stood out, crisp on the outside, meltingly fatty within. Ponzu, a citrus and vinegar-based soy sauce, is the perfect partner. If you can't find it, use soy sauce mixed with lime juice – entirely different but it works just as well.

Pork Belly with Ponzu Sauce

Mix the soy sauce, honey and lime juice in a non-reactive bowl, add the pork, cover and marinate in the fridge for 2–6 hours.

Preheat the oven to fan 160°C/325°F/Gas 4. Line a small roasting tin with foil and put the pork in the tin, fat side up, with its marinade. Cover the tin with foil and roast for 1½ hours.

Remove the foil, turn up the heat to fan 220°C/425°F/Gas 9 and roast for a further 15–20 minutes, until nicely browned and crisp. Serve with rice and ponzu sauce for dipping.

SERVES 6

6 tbsp soy sauce
4 tbsp runny honey
4 tbsp fresh lime juice (about 3 limes)
1kg/2lb 4oz rindless pork belly, cut into 5cm/2-inch chunks
boiled white rice, to serve
6 tbsp ponzu sauce, to serve

A Louisiana Cajun classic, this one-pot rolls wonderfully off the tongue. But all too often it can be a sorry, insipid shadow of its real self. I love Louisiana, which at times seems entirely separate not just from America, but from the modern world. This is a place where the best sausages, boudin blanc, come hot from petrol stations. And crawfish boils, deep in the bayou, are devoured to the chatter of the zydeco. I've spent many a happy hour downing Bloody Marys while cracking crawfish and blue crabs. Louisiana is the home of my favourite detective, James Lee Burke's Dave Robicheaux. And any state that has a cookbook called Who's your Mama, Are you Catholic and Can you make a Roux? *deserves to be adored. This jambalaya, starting off with the usual Cajun 'Holy Trinity' of onions, peppers and celery, tries to capture the slightly spiced charm of this down-home-in-the-bayou dish.*

Jambalaya

SERVES 6

12 skinless, boneless chicken
    thighs, halved
sea salt and freshly ground
    black pepper
4 tbsp vegetable oil
200g/7oz cooked ham (I
    prefer smoked), cut into
    2.5cm/1-inch dice
3–4 large onions, chopped
3 celery stalks, chopped
4 garlic cloves, finely chopped
2 green peppers, deseeded and
    roughly chopped
700ml/1¼ pints chicken stock
big pinch of cayenne pepper
400g/14oz can of chopped
    tomatoes
2–3 tsp hot sauce, such as
    Tabasco
300g/10½oz long-grain white
    rice
handful of fresh parsley,
    roughly chopped
350–400g/12–14oz raw,
    peeled and deveined prawns
    (pink, North Atlantic ones)
125g/4½oz spring onions,
    chopped

Season the chicken with salt and pepper. Heat 3 tbsp oil in a large, heavy casserole over a high heat and brown the chicken so it hisses and sizzles like crazy. You want that extra layer of caramelised flavour. Remove the chicken and set aside.

Add the ham to the pan and brown all over, then set aside with the chicken.

Add the remaining oil to the pan, reduce the heat to medium and soften the onions, celery and garlic, scraping up any browned bits. Put the chicken and ham back in the pan, then add the green peppers, stock, cayenne pepper and tomatoes and simmer for 10 minutes.

Add the hot sauce, salt and pepper, to taste. Add the rice and bring to the boil. Reduce the heat to low and simmer uncovered for another 10 minutes, until the rice is cooked. Add the parsley, prawns and spring onions and cook for another 8–10 minutes, until the prawns are completely pink and the rice is tender, stirring occasionally. Serve hot.

'This is a true worker's dish', I was told by chef Giorgio Locatelli, as he packed pig's cheek, sausages and ear and ribs into a vast, bubbling pot. 'It's a winter classic from Lombardy, traditionally made just after the killing of the pigs. It's the bits left behind after all the expensive parts have long departed.' He smiles. 'There are big arguments about whether to use red or white wine. My mother uses red …'. He shrugs. 'When it comes to food in Italy, everyone always has a different view as to what makes a dish right. It shows the food culture's still strong.' A few minutes spent with Giorgio, and all's well in the world. After teaching me to make it, he told me to come back later – when I picked up a vast tray of this cabbage-enriched winter warmer.

Cassoeula

SERVES 6

2 pigs' trotters, split into quarters
250g/9oz pork rind
1 pig's ear, rinsed and cleaned with kitchen paper
25g/1oz butter
2 tbsp olive oil
2 large onions, roughly chopped
700g/1lb 9oz pork spare ribs, cut into two-rib pieces
500g/1lb 2oz pig's cheek
2 large carrots, roughly chopped
2 celery stalks, roughly chopped
2 tbsp tomato purée
175ml/6fl oz red wine
1 large Savoy cabbage (about 1kg/2lb 4oz), shredded
500g/1lb 2oz coarse-ground, 100% pork Italian sausages (or good-quality 80–90% pork sausages), cut into 4cm/1½-inch pieces
sea salt and freshly ground black pepper

Put the pigs' trotters, pork rind and pig's ear in a large pan, cover with 1.5 litres/2¾ pints water, then bring to the boil and simmer for 1 hour. Remove the trotters, rind and ear. Cut any excess fat off the rind and discard it, then cut the rind into 4cm/1½-inch squares and slice the ear into long, thin strips. Leave the stock to cool, and then put it in the fridge. When cold, remove the solidified fat.

Preheat the oven to fan 140°C/275°F/Gas 2. Melt the butter and oil in a large, heavy casserole, add the onion and cook for about 10 minutes, until soft but not brown. Add the trotters, rind and ear and cook for a few minutes, then add the ribs and cook for 10 minutes, stirring frequently so the meat doesn't stick to the bottom of the pan.

Add the cheeks and cook for 5 minutes over a medium–high heat. Add the carrots, celery and tomato purée and cook for 2 minutes. Whack up the heat and add the wine. Let it reduce until thick and sticky, then pour in the reserved stock and make sure everything is covered. If not, top up with water to cover. Bring to a simmer, then cover the pan, transfer to the oven and cook for 2 hours. Add water if the liquid gets too low.

Add the cabbage and sausage pieces, stir, and cook for another 30–40 minutes. Season to taste and serve with lots of crusty bread. Or polenta.

There's no hiding with this baby. Pork, salt and pepper. That's it. And that's why it must be the very best meat you can afford. Cheap, intensively farmed pig means a grim, mealy mouthful. And grim, grey soggy crackling, as commercially produced pigs are bred to grow fast and lean. Get the butcher to score the skin for you. And lots of salt means good crisp crackling too.

Slow-Roasted Shoulder of Pork

Preheat the oven to fan 220°C/425°F/Gas 9. If your pork is rolled, snip off the string and unroll it. Pat the rind dry with kitchen paper, then score it deeply if it hasn't been done already, and rub it with salt and pepper. Place it in a roasting tin.

Roast for 30 minutes, until the rind is well on the way to crackling, then reduce the oven temperature to fan 140°C/275°F/Gas 2 and roast for 3½ hours, or until the pork is very tender but still juicy.

Leave to rest for 15 minutes. Carve into thick slices and serve hot.

SERVES 6

1.8–2kg/4–4½lb boneless
   shoulder of pork, with rind
1 heaped tbsp sea salt flakes
freshly ground black pepper

A classic Iberian dish, the clams add their sweet charms to small chunks of pig. Lard is the traditional cooking fat, but olive oil works fine too.

Pork with Clams

Put the meat in a non-reactive bowl with 5 tbsp of the wine, the paprika, bay leaf, half the garlic and a big pinch of salt and pepper, cover and leave in the fridge for at least 1 hour, or overnight.

Wash the clams in cold water and discard any that remain open when you tap them firmly.

Tip the pork into a colander over a large bowl to collect the marinade; leave to drain while you make the tomato sauce.

In a large heavy pan, heat 2 tbsp olive oil, then cook the onions and the remaining garlic until soft and golden. Add the tomatoes, season to taste and cook over a low heat for 10 minutes, stirring occasionally.

Pat the pork dry with kitchen paper. Heat the remaining oil in a large non-stick frying pan and cook the pork in three batches over a high heat until nicely browned but not quite cooked through. As each batch of pork is browned, transfer it to a plate using a slotted spoon.

Tip the marinade liquid into the frying pan, add the remaining wine and reduce to 6–7 tbsp. As it simmers, skim the froth from the top of the liquid. Return the pork to the reduced liquid.

Add the clams to the bubbling tomato sauce, cover and cook hard for 4–5 minutes, depending on size, until all are open. Discard any that do not open. Add the pork and liquid, scatter with parsley and serve hot, with bread and a wedge of lemon.

SERVES 4

2 small pork tenderloins (400g/14oz each), trimmed of sinew and cut into 2cm/¾-inch chunks

½ bottle (37.5cl) of dry white wine

2 heaped tsp hot paprika

1 bay leaf

4 garlic cloves, thinly sliced

sea salt and freshly ground black pepper

1kg/2lb 4oz live palourde or carpetshell clams in shells

3 tbsp olive oil

2 onions, sliced

4 tomatoes, peeled, deseeded and finely chopped

handful of fresh parsley, roughly chopped

sourdough bread, to serve

1 lemon, cut into wedges, to serve

Cheese meets bacon – a simple and magnificent snack match.

Gruyère Bacon

SERVES 4 AS A SNACK

16 rashers of smoked streaky bacon, rind removed

60g/2¼oz Gruyère, finely grated

60g/2¼oz fine dry white breadcrumbs

Preheat the grill to maximum. Lay the bacon on a wire rack over a baking sheet and place under the grill for 4–5 minutes.

Mix together the Gruyère and breadcrumbs. Dip the bacon in the cheese mixture to coat it on both sides. Turn the grill down to medium, put the bacon back under the grill and cook until crisp and golden, turning once – about 6 minutes. Drain on kitchen paper and serve hot.

Gammon steak and fried egg. Hmm... but I reckon the 'g' word is part of the reason we tend to steer clear of this fine cut. Too many memories of school gammon, with all the charm of a salt-lick block. The difference between gammon and ham is important. While the latter is made from the whole back leg, cut from the carcass and cured separately, gammon is cured as part of a side of bacon. It also makes a perfect burger filling, topped with an oozing egg.

Ham and Egg Burger

Heat a large griddle pan for about 10 minutes. Toast the buns on the pan, then set aside.

Cook the gammon steaks in the griddle pan for about 2–3 minutes on each side, until done. Keep warm.

In a small saucepan over a low heat, stir the honey, apple juice and mustard until smooth, then increase the heat and simmer until reduced and slightly thickened. Pour over the gammon steaks.

Heat the butter and oil in a frying pan, add the eggs and cook until the whites are just set and the yolk is still soft.

Lay a gammon steak on each bun, top with an egg, then a big spoonful of coleslaw and the top of the bun.

SERVES 4

4 burger buns, split
4 gammon steaks (about 200g/7oz each), snipped at regular intervals through the fat to stop it curling up during cooking
4 tbsp runny honey
4 tbsp good apple juice
1 tbsp English mustard
2 tbsp unsalted butter
1 tbsp sunflower oil
4 eggs
sea salt and freshly ground black pepper
200g/7oz coleslaw (*see* page 203), to serve

Laab, or larp, *is one of my favourite dishes, originally just raw meat with chillies. It's the national dish of Laos, and hugely popular in the north of Thailand (which was once part of the same kingdom anyway), where they have their own endless and generally gutsy takes on it. In Chiang Mai in particular the dish can get very gutsy indeed. This Burmese version is slightly different, using a complete spice paste. It's a recipe from the Shan people of Burma and north-eastern Thailand and works well with chicken or pork. Dry-frying the garlic gives it a smoky depth that immediately reminds me of the region. If you can do it over coals, then so much the better.*

Shan Pork Laab

SERVES 4

1 tbsp groundnut or sunflower oil

8 Thai (or 2 banana) shallots, thinly sliced

500g/1lb 2oz minced pork or chicken

6 spring onions, sliced diagonally

large handful of coriander leaves, roughly chopped

1 lime, halved

1–2 tbsp toasted rice powder (buy from an Asian food shop or make your own)

steamed sticky rice, to serve

SPICE PASTE

8 garlic cloves, skin on

1 tsp sea salt flakes

2 lemongrass stalks, chopped

20g/¾oz fresh galangal, peeled and chopped

5 dried Thai red chillies

1–2 tbsp groundnut or sunflower oil

To make the spice paste, toast the garlic in a dry pan over a medium–high heat for 6–8 minutes, until the skins blacken. Or cook over coals. Remove the skin and either finely chop, or chop roughly the garlic and throw into a small blender.

If using a blender, add the rest of the paste ingredients and blitz to make a thick paste. Otherwise, use a mortar and pestle, beginning with the garlic and salt, then adding the other ingredients (finely chopped) until you have a thick paste.

Heat a large, heavy pan, add the oil and cook the shallots for a couple of minutes. Add the spice paste and cook until fragrant. Add the pork mince and cook for 2–3 minutes, stirring frequently, until browned. Add the spring onions and coriander. Sprinkle with a good squeeze of lime juice and the rice powder and serve with sticky rice.

Toasted Rice Powder

Heat a wok or small heavy-bottomed pan over a medium–low heat, add a couple of handfuls of uncooked white rice (ideally sticky rice) and dry-fry for about 3 minutes, stirring frequently with a wooden spoon, until the rice starts to toast and give off a biscuity smell. Transfer the rice to a bowl to cool. Grind the cooled rice in a coffee grinder or pound in a mortar and pestle to a fine powder. Set aside.

Lamb chops, cut thin from a young beast, grilled over coals. You eat them as the fat still spits and sizzles, burning your fingers as you go. Hence 'scottadito', or 'finger searing'. Obviously, you can do them in a grill pan but it rather misses the point. You want the whiff of wood smoke, and that charred, blistered fat. I've eaten these in Rome made from abbacchio, *about the only time spring lamb is worth eating. They were smeared with* lardo *(cured pork back fat), heavily seasoned and thrown over the coals. If no* lardo *is to hand, use olive oil and a very heavy hand with the salt and pepper.*

Scottadito di Agnello

Light your barbecue and wait until the coals are white-hot. Rub the *lardo* onto the chops, then season like hell.

Grill for about a minute on each side, maybe two. Eat searing hot, with a squeeze of lemon and some bitter leaves.

SERVES 4

a piece of softened *lardo* (or a
   dribble of olive oil)
16 thin-cut lamb chops, ideally
   from a rack of lamb
sea salt and freshly ground
   black pepper
1 lemon, quartered
bitter salad leaves, to serve

Slow-cooked lamb, studded with garlic, surrounded by an adoring crowd of shallots, fennel and broad beans. This recipe is adapted from one by Bill Knott, the Financial Times's *Gannet, and a serious lunching companion. If broad beans aren't in season, use frozen.*

Slow-Cooked Lamb with Shallots, Fennel and Broad Beans

SERVES 6

1 shoulder of lamb (about 2kg/4lb 8oz) trimmed of excess fat

4 garlic cloves, each cut into 3 slices

sea salt and freshly ground black pepper

3 tbsp light olive oil

12 banana shallots, peeled, with the roots kept intact

1 fennel bulb, fairly thickly sliced

300ml/10fl oz dry white wine

500ml/18fl oz chicken stock (cube is fine)

1 tbsp chopped fresh thyme

1 tbsp white wine vinegar

2 bay leaves

1 tbsp pastis (or 2 tsp toasted fennel seeds)

150g/5½oz podded and peeled broad beans

75g/2¾oz anchovies preserved in salt, roughly chopped

2 tbsp roughly chopped fresh parsley

1 tbsp Dijon mustard

Preheat the oven to fan 160°C/325°F/Gas 4. Using a small sharp knife, make 12 little slits around the lamb and push a garlic slice into each one. Season the lamb liberally all over.

Heat the oil in a large frying pan, then sear the lamb until deep brown on all sides. Transfer it to a snug casserole dish.

Cook the shallots and fennel slices in the frying pan until slightly coloured, then add the wine and bubble away the alcohol. Add the stock, thyme, vinegar and bay leaves, simmer for a couple of minutes, then pour over the lamb. Cover with a tight-fitting lid and cook in the oven for 3 hours or so, turning after 1½ hours and adding a little more stock if needed. The lamb should be tender, but not completely soft. Leave to rest for 20 minutes. Spoon off any fat that has risen to the surface.

Remove the bones – they should pull out easily – then break the meat into chunks and pile in the middle of a warmed serving dish. Arrange the shallots and fennel around the lamb.

Put the juices in a wide saucepan over a high heat, add the pastis or fennel seeds, and bring back to the boil; if necessary, reduce to about 500ml/18fl oz. Add the broad beans, anchovies, parsley and mustard, then simmer gently for 2 minutes, until the beans are cooked. Taste and adjust the seasoning, then pour the beans and juices over the lamb and serve hot.

Nigel Howarth is one of Britain's finest cooks, and a fierce advocate of the produce of the North West. Alongside his old mates Reg Johnson and Paul Heathcote, they make up a mighty Lancastrian triumvirate. There are various versions of the Lancashire hotpot, but his is the best I've ever tasted. Here it is – it might seem a little cheffy, with all those different cuts of lamb – but it's not. Serve with pickled red cabbage.

Lancashire Hotpot

SERVES 4

200g/7oz boneless lamb
   shoulder, trimmed of excess
   fat and cut into 4cm/
   1½-inch pieces
150g/5½oz lamb leg steaks,
   cut into 4cm/1½-inch pieces
150g/5½oz lamb neck fillet,
   cut into 4cm/1½-inch pieces
pinch of caster sugar
sea salt and freshly ground
   black pepper
25g/1oz plain flour
4 lamb loin chops (100g/3½oz
   each)
2 tbsp olive oil
50g/1¾oz salted butter,
   melted
4 onions, thinly sliced
500g/1lb 2oz Golden Wonder
   or other floury potatoes,
   peeled and cut into
   2mm/¹⁄₁₆-inch thick slices
pinch of ground white pepper

Preheat the oven to fan 160°C/325°F/Gas 4. Season the meat with the sugar, ½ tsp salt and some black pepper. Toss with the flour and arrange in a heavy hotpot or casserole.

Season the loin chops. Heat the oil in a pan and sear the chops on all sides for 3–4 minutes, or until golden brown. Put them on top of the raw meat.

Heat 1 tbsp of the butter in a clean pan over a medium–low heat until foaming, add the onions with 1 tsp salt and cook for 2–3 minutes, or until soft but not browned. Spread the onions evenly over the lamb.

Put the potatoes in a bowl, add the remaining butter, season with 1 tsp salt and a pinch of white pepper, and mix well. Layer the sliced potatoes on top of the onions.

Bake the hotpot, covered, for 2 hours, removing the lid for the final 30 minutes.

To serve, divide among four bowls, making sure there's a chop in each bowl.

Mexican slow-cooked magic. You may think lamb an unlikely ingredient, but you'll find it all over Mexico. It's cooked in adobo, a vinegar-spiked chilli paste. But this isn't about heat, rather the flavour of dried chilli mixed with a good kick of vinegar.

Carnero Adobo

Put the lamb in a heavy-bottomed saucepan with half the garlic and onion, then add the coriander stalks, celery, peppercorns and bay leaf. Add just enough water to cover (about 1.5 litres/2½ pints), bring to the boil and skim off any scum. Reduce the heat to the merest simmer, cover the pan and cook for 2½–3 hours, until the meat is soft.

Remove the meat using a slotted spoon, strain the stock and set aside.

Put the chillies, cumin, oregano, vinegar, salt and remaining onion and garlic into a blender and purée to a smooth paste.

Heat the lard or oil over a low heat and cook the paste until it becomes wonderfully fragrant – about 5 minutes. Add the reserved stock until you have a loose, slightly runny sauce. Add the lamb and simmer for 15 minutes. Season with salt to taste, and serve hot, with fresh tortillas or rice.

SERVES 4

1kg/2lb 4oz boneless lamb shoulder, trimmed of excess fat and cut into 5cm/2-inch chunks

3 garlic cloves, finely chopped

1 large onion, cut into 12 wedges

4 coriander stalks

2 celery stalks, roughly chopped

5 black peppercorns

1 bay leaf

5 pasilla chillies (from www. coolchile.co.uk), soaked in just-boiled water for 20 minutes, drained and chopped

½ tsp cumin seeds, toasted until fragrant, then ground

½ tsp Mexican oregano (from www.coolchile.co.uk, or use European oregano)

3 tbsp red wine vinegar

½ tsp sea salt flakes, plus extra to taste

3 tbsp lard or vegetable oil

tortillas or boiled rice, to serve

These Yang Rou Chuan *offered welcome relief from the dried seahorses and snakeskins on skewers at the tourist markets in Beijing. They're actually a speciality of the Xinjiang province, in north-west China, a place of bitter winters, where lamb is a staple. Simple, smoky and scented with cumin. This really should be done on the barbecue, as the chilli fumes will make you cough. Or turn the extractor fan up really high, to suck away the fumes.*

North-Western Chinese Lamb Skewers

SERVES 4

600g/1lb 5oz boneless leg of lamb, trimmed of excess fat and cut into 2.5cm/1-inch chunks

3 tbsp cumin seeds, toasted until fragrant, then ground in a mortar and pestle

2 tbsp dried chilli flakes

1 tbsp sea salt

3 tbsp groundnut or sunflower oil

wedges of lemon or lime, to serve

Soak 12 wooden skewers in water for at least 30 minutes. Light your barbecue and wait until the coals are white-hot, or heat your griddle pan until it's smoking hot.

Put about three pieces of meat on each skewer.

Mix the cumin, chilli and salt on a plate. Put the oil on another plate. Roll the skewers of meat in the oil, then in the spices, until well coated.

Grill for 3–4 minutes on each side; the meat should still be pink inside. Leave to rest for a minute, then serve with a squeeze of lemon or lime.

I once had a tagine, the cone-topped earthenware vessel after which this North African dish is named. It looked suitably exotic, but I only used it once before it was relegated, lonely and unloved, to the back of the cupboard. It has long passed on to some Oxfam beyond the stars. But this dish can easily be cooked in a wide, shallow pot. It's really just a stew, and is traditionally served with flatbread, as couscous is a separate dish. But I like couscous with this. If fresh artichokes aren't in season, you can use canned (a 400g/14oz can contains eight artichoke hearts) or bottled.

Lemon and Artichoke Tagine

SERVES 6

4 tbsp olive oil

about 1kg/2lb 4oz shoulder of lamb, trimmed of excess fat, meat taken off the bone and cut into 5cm/2-inch chunks

3 red onions, roughly chopped

5 garlic cloves, crushed

1 small pickled lemon, cut into 2cm/¾-inch pieces (pips discarded)

sea salt

½ tsp ground black pepper

5cm/2-inch cinnamon stick

½ tsp ground ginger

1–2 tbsp harissa paste (optional)

12 artichoke hearts (fresh, bottled or canned), cut in half

handful of fresh parsley, roughly chopped

Heat 2 tbsp oil in a large, wide, shallow pot over a medium–high heat and brown the meat all over for about 10 minutes. Remove from the pot with a slotted spoon and set aside.

Reduce the heat to medium, add the remaining oil and cook the onions and garlic for 10 minutes, until soft.

Return the meat to the pot, together with the lemon, salt, pepper, cinnamon, ginger and harissa (if using) and stir, then add water to cover everything by 5cm/2 inches. Bring to the boil, then reduce the heat to low, cover and simmer gently for 40 minutes, until the meat is almost tender.

If using fresh artichokes, add them and continue to simmer, uncovered, for a further 40 minutes. If using bottled or canned artichokes, simmer the meat for an additional 20–30 minutes before adding the artichokes, then simmer for a final 10–15 minutes.

Remove the cinnamon stick, sprinkle with parsley and serve with couscous.

To make this classic French dish truly exceptional, try to hunt down a bird that's well past its prime. You want an ageing Lothario, a cock that has strutted round the yard and had the hens falling at his feet. But these can be difficult to find. And as Elizabeth David says, 'It doesn't have to be a cockerel.' I've adapted this recipe from the one in her French Country Cooking; *she's entirely unconcerned with petty specifics such as oven temperatures, but her prose sparkles. And the end result is suitably robust.*

Coq au Vin

Preheat the oven to fan 150°C/300°F/Gas 3. Season the bird inside and out and cover with the lemon juice.

In a large, heavy pan, melt 25g/1oz butter with the oil over a medium–high heat and brown the bird all over. This will take at least 10 minutes, as you want a caramelised, mahogany-coloured skin.

Whack up the heat and pour in the brandy. It should catch light. When the flames have died down, stir to deglaze the pan, then add most of the wine, keeping aside a small glass – about 125ml/4fl oz. If the bird has giblets, add them too (leaving out the liver). Bring the liquid to a simmer, cover and cook in the oven for about 1½ hours.

In a small pan, heat 15g/½oz butter and brown the onions for 4–5 minutes, then sprinkle over the sugar and the small glass of wine. Let the wine reduce for about 4 minutes, swirling the pan until the sauce clings to the onions.

Remove the chicken from the oven, add the onions and simmer for 15 minutes, until they are tender and the sauce has thickened.

Heat the remaining butter in a small pan over a medium–high heat and cook the mushrooms for about 4 minutes, until browned and soft. Add them to the chicken.

Remove the chicken from the pan. Check it is cooked through by inserting a skewer into the thickest part; any juices should be clear. Leave to rest for 10 minutes, then carve it. If the sauce is not quite thick enough, reduce it over a high heat, then taste and adjust the seasoning. Serve the chicken, onions and mushrooms with some of the hot sauce spooned over.

SERVES 4–6

1 large chicken, the best you can afford
sea salt and freshly ground black pepper
juice of ½ lemon
55g/2oz unsalted butter
1 tbsp sunflower oil
100ml/3½fl oz brandy
75cl bottle of red wine
20 baby onions, peeled
1 tsp caster sugar
250g/9oz button or chestnut mushrooms

If Cajun is the Acadian-accented food of the Louisiana countryside, then Creole is its scent-drenched and sophisticated urban cousin. It's rich and sumptuous — often overwhelmingly so. What they share is their adoration of the roux, which both thickens and flavours. Some recipes call for a mahogany-coloured roux, but this one is medium red-brown, so you cook it until the colour starts to change. Have faith, as this takes time. If it burns and black specks appear, then throw it out and start again.

Creole Chicken Stew with Mustard Dumplings

In a large, heavy-bottomed saucepan, make the red-brown roux. Melt the butter, then add the flour, a third at a time, whisking until smooth before adding more. Cook over a medium–low heat, stirring often, for 10–20 minutes, until beginning to colour.

Add the onions, pepper, celery and tomatoes and cook for 10 minutes, until soft, stirring often to ensure the roux doesn't burn.

Bring the stock to the boil in a separate pan, then add to the roux and vegetables in batches, stirring as you go. Add the paprika, mustard, cayenne, white pepper and a big pinch of salt and simmer gently for 25 minutes. Add the chicken meat and simmer for 5 minutes.

Meanwhile, to make the dumplings, mix the flour, baking powder, mustard, cayenne and a big pinch of salt in a bowl. In another bowl, combine the eggs, butter and 3 tbsp milk. Pour the wet ingredients onto the dry to make a soft, spongy dough, adding a little more milk if necessary, then add the parsley and stir to mix evenly.

Dust your hands with flour and form the dough into small dumplings, dropping them directly onto the stew. Cover tightly with a lid and simmer for 10 minutes.

Serve hot, with parsley and pork scratchings sprinkled over the top.

SERVES 4

40g/1½oz butter
20g/¾oz plain flour
3 onions, roughly chopped
1 large green pepper, deseeded and chopped
3 celery stalks, chopped
4 tomatoes, deseeded and roughly chopped
1 litre/1¾ pints chicken stock
1 tsp hot smoked paprika
½ tsp mustard powder
½ tsp cayenne pepper
¼ tsp ground white pepper
sea salt
1kg/2lb 4oz roasted chicken meat, skinned and cut into 3cm/1¼-inch wide strips
handful of fresh parsley, roughly chopped
50g/1¾oz pork scratchings (Mr Trotter's), crushed

MUSTARD DUMPLINGS
150g/5½oz plain flour
½ tsp baking powder
1 tbsp mustard powder
½ tsp cayenne pepper
2 eggs, beaten
60g/2¼oz butter, melted
3–4 tbsp milk
handful of fresh parsley, roughly chopped

I'd swim oceans and crawl across continents for just one taste of these. Well, I like to think I would, because they are one of the great American snacks. Disputes rage as to exactly which restaurant in Buffalo, New York, they hail from. The strongest claim is from the Anchor Bar, owned by Teressa and Frank Bellissimo. One night in 1964, their son, Dominic, arrived late with a gang of friends who needed feeding. Teressa grabbed some wings, deep-fried them and tossed them in a buttery hot sauce. Dominic has a different take, claiming that his mother invented them for a full bar on a Friday night; being mainly Catholic, and not eating meat on a Friday, the punters were hungry and Dominic thought the wings would make a fine treat for the early hours of Saturday morning. Whatever the truth, the wings must be deep-fried. And coated with a mixture of butter and hot sauce. Tradition has it that they're served with a blue cheese dip and celery sticks. It's the part I always leave, but I've included the recipe all the same.

Proper Buffalo Wings

SERVES 4

sunflower oil for deep-frying
20 chicken wings
100g/3½oz butter
150ml/5fl oz hot sauce, such as Tabasco, Crystal or Frank's Red Hot Original
5 celery stalks, spilt in half then cut into batons, to serve

BLUE CHEESE DIP
150g/5½oz soft blue cheese
300ml/10fl oz sour cream
squeeze of lemon

In a deep pan, heat the oil to 180°C/350°F, or until a cube of bread browns in 30 seconds. Deep-fry the wings, in batches, until golden brown and cooked through with no sign of pink in the juices, 5–10 minutes. Drain on kitchen paper and keep warm.

Melt the butter in a pan, add the hot sauce and stir vigorously until smooth. Add the wings and coat each and every one.

To make the dip, mash up the blue cheese with the cream and lemon juice. Serve the dip in a bowl alongside the chicken wings and celery.

I first tried this dish in Luang Prabang, the seductively somnolent ancient capital of Laos. Life there moves slower than the Mekong in dry season, but the food was a revelation. This royal dish is not as hot as you might imagine, the chilli tamed by the coconut milk. If you can be bothered to grate a fresh coconut yourself, then so much the better. Otherwise, canned will do.

Laotian Chilli Chicken

SERVES 4

milk of 1 ripe coconut (see method), or 400ml/14fl oz can of unsweetened coconut milk mixed with 200ml/ 7fl oz cold water

groundnut or sunflower oil for frying (or lard, if you want to be authentic)

6 Thai (or 2 banana) shallots, thinly sliced

2 chicken legs, divided into drumsticks and thighs

2 chicken breasts, halved

1 onion, thinly sliced

2 tbsp fish sauce

6–8 long dried red chillies, halved, deseeded and white part scraped away, soaked in cold water for 20 minutes, drained

10 spring onions, sliced diagonally, including most of the green

freshly ground black pepper

handful of fresh coriander leaves, roughly chopped

steamed sticky rice, to serve

If using fresh coconut, grate the flesh, mix with a little water, then put into a piece of muslin and squeeze into a bowl. Add a little more water to the flesh and squeeze again. Set aside.

Pour 2cm/¾ inch oil into a saucepan, heat to around 170°C/340°F, or until a cube of bread turns golden in 30 seconds, then deep-fry the shallots for 3–4 minutes, until golden. Using a slotted spoon, transfer to a plate lined with kitchen paper. You may need to do this in two batches.

Heat 3 tbsp oil or lard in a wok or frying pan over a medium-high heat, add the chicken and onion and cook, turning once or twice, until the chicken is golden. Transfer the chicken breasts to a plate. Add the coconut milk and fish sauce to the pan and top up with enough water to almost cover the chicken legs. Stir in the chillies and cook over a low heat for 10 minutes.

Return the chicken breasts to the pan and simmer gently for 10 minutes, until cooked through, with no sign of pink in the juices when a skewer is inserted into the thickest part. Add a little more water if the sauce becomes too thick.

Stir in the spring onions and cook for 2 minutes. Season with pepper and sprinkle with the fried shallots and the coriander just before serving. Serve with sticky rice.

One of the most abused dishes in the entire Far Eastern canon, this deserves to be done properly.
So forget all those dried-up clumps of rubbery poultry, served in a peanut sauce so sweet it
makes your teeth ache. You'll find satay all over South-East Asia; this is a Thai version. Like all
Thai food, it is about balance, in this case sweet and salty. If you can cook these over charcoal,
you'll get close to a taste of the real thing. If not, use a ridged cast-iron griddle pan.

Thai Chicken Satay

MAKES 24 SKEWERS

12 large skinless, boneless
   chicken thighs

MARINADE

1 tbsp coriander seeds, toasted

1 tsp cumin seeds, toasted

1 lemongrass stalk, chopped

250ml/9fl oz coconut cream

3 tbsp fish sauce

20g/¾oz fresh galangal,
   peeled and chopped

1 tsp ground turmeric

4 bird's-eye chillies, chopped

2 garlic cloves, chopped

2 tbsp groundnut oil

1 tbsp palm (or caster) sugar

DIPPING SAUCE

1 tbsp coriander seeds, toasted

1 tbsp cumin seeds, toasted

5 dried red chillies, soaked in
   just-boiled water for
   20 minutes, finely chopped

½ lemongrass stalk, chopped

15g/½oz fresh galangal,
   peeled and chopped

3 Thai shallots, chopped

3 garlic cloves, chopped

2 tsp groundnut oil

350ml/12fl oz coconut cream

1 tbsp palm (or caster) sugar

150g/5½oz unsalted toasted
   peanuts, finely ground

1 tbsp fish sauce

1 tbsp fresh lime juice

To make the marinade, put all the ingredients in a food
processor and blitz until smooth.

Put the chicken in a non-reactive bowl, spoon over the
marinade, and cover. Marinate in the fridge for at least 2 hours,
or preferably overnight.

To make the dipping sauce, put the coriander seeds and cumin
seeds in a mortar and pestle and grind to a powder. Put them
in a food processor, add the chillies, lemongrass, galangal,
shallots and garlic and blitz until as smooth as possible. Add
the oil and 1–2 tbsp water if the paste seems too dry.

Heat a heavy-bottomed pan and cook the paste over a
medium–high heat for 1–2 minutes, until fragrant. Add the
coconut cream, reduce the heat, and stir. Add the sugar and
simmer over a low heat for 5 minutes, then add the peanuts
and cook for 1 minute. Add the fish sauce and lime juice, then
cover and leave to sit for 1 hour before serving.

Soak 24 wooden skewers in water for at least 30 minutes.
Light your barbecue and wait until the coals are white-hot, or
heat your griddle pan until it's smoking hot. Trim any excess
fat off the chicken, then cut each thigh lengthwise into four
long strips.

Thread two pieces of chicken onto each skewer and grill,
turning often, for 4–5 minutes, or until cooked through with
no sign of pink in the juices when the largest piece is cut in
half. Serve hot, with the dipping sauce.

'When it comes to fried chicken', decrees food writer James Villas, 'let's not beat about the bush for one second. To know about fried chicken you have to have been weaned and reared on it in the South. Period.' So I obviously don't know about fried chicken. But I love the stuff, with its crisp, dry, burnished shell concealing the succulent chicken within. One of my favourite restaurants is a small place, little more than a shed, on the outskirts of Nashville, Tennessee. It's called Prince's Hot Chicken, and it specialises in spicy chicken, fried in vast iron skillets. Cayenne pepper gives it its kick. You can get it from Mild to Extra Hot. Beware the Extra Hot. As the Mayor of Nashville once told me while chowing down on a thigh, 'This ain't talking food.' As that blast of pure capsaicin hits the mouth, you realise this is somewhat of an understatement. It's so hot it makes thinking hurt. This is my version, to be served with pickles and atop cheap white bread.

Fried Chicken (with thanks to Prince's Hot Chicken)

Cut each chicken into eight pieces: remove the legs and thighs, and separate. Cut the wings off, leaving the last section attached to the breast (save the tips and middle sections for stock). Cut away and discard the backbone. Cut each breast in half down the breast bone.

Mix the salt with 1 litre/1¾ pints cold water, add the chicken, cover and leave in the fridge to soak for 1 hour. Remove and pat dry. Mix the buttermilk with the hot sauce and a big pinch of salt. Add the chicken, cover and leave in the fridge to soak for 1 hour. In a large bowl, mix the flour, cayenne pepper, salt and pepper.

Heat the oil, about 8cm/3 inches deep, in a heavy-bottomed pan or, better still, a blackened and battered iron skillet, until sizzling but not shimmering and spitting – around 150°C/300°F. Remove the chicken from the marinade, shake well, then coat one piece in the spiced flour, shaking off any excess. Repeat with the rest of the chicken. Deep-fry a few pieces at a time (they need space, so don't crowd them), turning once or twice, until golden, about 8–10 minutes. Drain on kitchen paper and lay atop a slice of cheap white bread. Serve with cheap bottled sweet pickles.

SERVES 4, OR 8 AS A SNACK

2 small (about 1kg/2lb 4oz) whole chickens
100g/3½oz fine sea salt
600ml/20fl oz buttermilk
4 tsp hot sauce, such as Tabasco or Crystal
100g/3½oz plain flour
1–4 tbsp cayenne pepper (1 for mild, 4 for hellish hot)
pinch of salt
generous grinding of black pepper
about 500ml/18fl oz groundnut or vegetable oil
white bread, to serve
bottled sweet pickles, to serve

The quail is an underrated bird. The farmed ones can be very bland indeed. But with a little wallow in a marinade, and a few minutes spent sprawled over coals, they're transformed into something rather wonderful. This recipe is inspired by Mien Tay, an excellent Vietnamese restaurant in Kingsland Road, east London. You want the skin sticky and charred, the flesh sweet and succulent. And don't even think about knives and forks. There's no place for bourgeois niceties here.

Grilled Spiced Quail

SERVES 4 (OR 2 HUNGRY FOLK)

4 large quail
sea salt

MARINADE

1 tbsp groundnut or sunflower oil
juice of 2 limes
2 tbsp runny honey
1 tbsp dark soy sauce
1 tbsp fish sauce
pinch of ground cinnamon
½ lemongrass stalk, finely chopped

DIPPING SALT

1 heaped tbsp sea salt
1 tsp ground white pepper
2 bird's-eye chillies, finely chopped
2 limes, halved

Mix all the marinade ingredients together in a small pan over a low heat. Stir until smooth. Leave to cool completely.

Put the quail on a chopping board, breast side down, and split each bird lengthwise along the backbone. Open it out and press down with the heel of your hand to flatten. Turn the quail over so the skin side is up and press again so the bird is totally flat.

Put the quail in a large, resealable plastic bag, pour in the marinade, and seal. Marinate in the fridge for at least 1 hour – overnight is better – turning halfway through.

Light your barbecue and wait until the coals are white-hot, or heat your griddle pan until it's smoking hot. Take the birds out of the bag, season with salt, then grill, skin-side down, for about 5 minutes, until the skin is browned but not burnt. Turn and cook for another 5–6 minutes. Check the quail is cooked by piercing the thigh with a skewer; the juices should be golden, not pink. Leave to rest for 3–5 minutes.

While the birds are resting, mix the salt, pepper and chillies for the dipping salt; divide among four small bowls. Serve the quail with a bowl of dipping salt and half a lime, for eaters to mix with the spicy salt.

I once spent the morning in the kitchen of HKK, a very swish Cantonese place in the City. It was vast, gleaming and spotless, the extraction system so powerful it could rip the words straight from your mouth. But I was here for the special Cantonese duck cooked by chef Tong, a man of few words. 'The duck is the star here,' was one of the rare pearls that fell from his lips. 'Not like the Peking style, where pancakes, sauce and spring onions get in the way.' Quite. But despite what chef Tong says, this goes rather well with pancakes, spring onions and a dribble of that thick, sweet sauce. You want a really good duck, either one from Reg Johnson in Goosnargh, near Preston in Lancashire, or a Cherry Valley duck, specially reared for this sort of recipe.

Cantonese Roast Duck

Preheat the oven to fan 150°C/300°F/Gas 3. Wash the duck in cold water, then dry carefully with kitchen paper.

Mix together the ingredients for the seasoning salt and rub it inside the duck. Stuff the ginger and halved spring onions into the cavity. If you have metal skewers, you can use them to secure the cavity. If not, don't worry.

Hang the duck above a bowl. Mix the glazing syrup ingredients with 50ml/2fl oz cold water in a small pan and bring to the boil. Ladle the hot syrup over the duck, repeating four or five times and tipping the excess syrup from the bowl underneath the duck back into the hot pan each time.

Put the duck on its back on a wire rack in a roasting tin and roast for 1 hour. Take out of the oven and drain off any fat that has collected in the tin (keep it for roast potatoes). Turn the duck over onto its breast and cook for another hour. Drain off the fat once more. Turn the oven up to fan 200°C/400°F/Gas 7 and roast the duck for a final 20 minutes, or until the skin is crisp.

Leave to rest for 15 minutes, then carve and serve hot. With pancakes, sliced spring onions and a dribble of hoisin sauce if you like.

SERVES 4

1 duck (about 1.8kg/4lb)
2 thick slices of fresh ginger, peeled and bashed once or twice with the thick side of a knife
3 spring onions, halved
steamed Chinese pancakes, to serve
spring onions, thinly sliced, to serve
hoisin sauce, to serve (optional)

SEASONING SALT
2 tsp fine sea salt
2 tsp caster sugar
½ tsp five-spice powder

GLAZING SYRUP
100g/3½oz maltose (available from Chinese supermarkets)
100ml/3½fl oz white wine vinegar

Less MEAT

This chapter is a place where the 'lesser' cuts – thighs, cured pieces of pork, mince and scraps of meat – play their role. You can still use good-quality meat, but you don't have to splash out on fillets and ribs or tenderloins of pork. A fragrant Chicken Lahori curry (*see* page 106), using just chicken stock and a few bits of thigh. Or a proper Cornish pasty (*see* page 72), with small pieces of skirt. It is all about getting the joys of meat, for a fraction of the price.

And it's here you'll find meat sharing the page with all manner of carbohydrates. Sheets of pasta in a rather English take on lasagne (*see* page 74), soft noodles that gently meld with charred pork (*see* page 79), bean stews (*see* pages 83, 86, 93 and 94), bread, potatoes and bulgur wheat.

Many of the dishes are slow cooked, meaning you can use all those wonderful, cheaper cuts (shoulder of hogget, shin of beef, ham hock) that relish a long stew in the oven. What starts off as tough and unappealing relaxes and starts to fall about in great luscious strands. The more work a particular piece of the beast has done, the less suited it is to quick cooking.

Spice, too, plays a key role, turning the everyday into the extraordinary. God, I love spice. A few pinches of chilli in a Neapolitan ragù (*see* page 76), the Cape Malay exotica of Bobotie – cumin and coriander seeds, turmeric and cayenne pepper (*see* page 75), fresh chillies bunged into Mexican *frijoles* (*see* page 83), the charms of cinnamon in kibbeh nayyeh (*see* page 98).

Dishes appear from all over the world: Mexico, Pakistan, South Africa, Italy, Vietnam, Laos and the UK. But this is meat as character actor, supporting role, essential but discreet. Less meat, but no less carnivorous joy.

I was a judge on a TV programme a couple of years back, looking for Britain's favourite dish. It was huge fun making the programme. One of the high points was meeting Eunice Woolcock, a wonderful 91-year-old Cornish lady who made the best pasties I'd ever tasted. Just sublime. There's lots of guff talked about pasties, but because they were hardy and portable they were originally food for the tin miners. The key is not cooking anything first. And no fancy ingredients, either. No mucking about, just raw skirt or chuck steak, raw potato and swede, lots of pepper and proper pastry. As Eunice would say, 'There's Cornish pasty. And that's it. The rest are just pasties.' This recipe is adapted from her's.

Cornish Pasty

MAKES 2 PASTIES

PASTRY
225g/8oz plain flour, plus
    extra for dusting
pinch of salt
50g/1¾oz lard, chilled and
    diced
50g/1¾oz hard margarine,
    chilled and cut into cubes

FILLING
1 potato (150g/5½oz), peeled
    and thinly sliced
50g/1¾oz swede, peeled and
    thinly sliced
115g/4oz beef skirt or chuck
    steak, finely diced
¼ small onion, thinly sliced
salt and ground white pepper
milk or beaten egg to glaze

To make the pastry, mix together the flour and salt, and rub in the fats. Gradually stir in 2–3 tbsp water and bring everything together with your hands to form a smooth, pliable dough. Divide the dough into two balls.

Preheat the oven to fan 180°C/350°F/Gas 6. Line a baking sheet with baking parchment.

On a floured work surface, roll out one ball of dough to form a circle about 20cm/8 inches across. Slightly off centre of the circle, place a layer of potato, then a layer of swede. Add half the beef, then half the onion, then a pinch of salt and plenty of pepper. Finally, add another thin layer of potato, to stop the meat from drying out. Carefully fold the pastry over and crimp the edges together. Place on the lined baking sheet. Repeat to make the second pasty.

Glaze with a little milk or egg, and make a small hole in the top. Bake for 40 minutes, until golden brown. Serve hot or cold.

Yeah, yeah, I know that the Italians only use a minuscule amount of ragù, and the real thing is an elegant, almost dainty dish of pasta and restraint. But bugger that. I want torrents of meat sauce, rivers of béchamel and a good few sheets of pasta too. In short, the version I grew up with, with the sagging gut and hanky tied around its head. This is real comfort food, a mass of wonderful stodge that never ceases to delight. This is English lasagne. Despite the seemingly vast size of the recipe, fear not. It's very simple, even if it does manage to soil pretty much every pan you own. The ragù alla Bolognese is rich, deeply flavoured and perfect for lasagne.

Lasagne

SERVES 6

300g/10½oz fresh or dried lasagne

50g/1¾oz Parmesan, finely grated

RAGÙ ALLA BOLOGNESE

50g/1¾oz butter

2 tbsp olive oil

1 onion, finely chopped

1 carrot, finely chopped

1 celery stalk, finely chopped

4 chicken livers, trimmed and finely chopped

250g/9oz pancetta or unsmoked bacon, finely chopped

600g/1lb 5oz minced beef, pork or veal, or a mixture

300ml/10fl oz red wine

sea salt and freshly ground black pepper

4 tbsp tomato purée

400ml/14fl oz fresh beef stock (*see* page 227)

150ml/5fl oz double cream

BÉCHAMEL SAUCE

600ml/20fl oz full-fat milk

60g/2¼oz butter, plus extra to butter the dish

60g/2¼oz plain flour

grating of fresh nutmeg

To make the ragù, heat the butter and oil in a deep saucepan over a medium heat, add the vegetables and fry until they soften and brown lightly. Add the livers and cook until pink. Add the pancetta and minced meat and fry until the meat colours. Add the wine, simmer until it evaporates, then add salt and pepper, tomato purée and a little of the stock. Cover and cook over a low heat for 1½ hours, stirring occasionally and gradually stirring in all the stock.

Stir in the cream and cook, uncovered, until slightly reduced, about 10 minutes. Set aside.

To make the béchamel, heat the milk until it's just about to boil, then set aside. Melt the butter in a saucepan and stir in the flour over a medium heat, until you have a smooth, just golden roux. Gradually add the hot milk, stirring all the time (I use a mini-whisk with a horseshoe-shaped twist of wire at the end) until the sauce is thick and velvety smooth. When it comes to the boil, stop stirring and cook gently for about 10 minutes. Add nutmeg and salt and pepper to taste. Set aside.

Preheat the oven to fan 170°C/340°F/Gas 5. If using dried lasagne, cook it in a large pan of boiling water until al dente. Drain and rinse briefly under cold water to remove excess starch. Butter a 2.5–3 litre/4½–5 pint rectangular baking dish and add about one-third of the ragù. Cover with a layer of pasta, then splodge in about one-third of the béchamel. Repeat the layers twice more. Sprinkle the Parmesan over the top, then bake for 40 minutes, until the cheese is bubbling. Serve hot.

Born in Indonesia, and shipped into South Africa via the Dutch East India Company, the Cape-Malay bobotie is the South African equivalent of shepherd's pie. Albeit with a custard topping and a whiff of exotic spices. Traditional recipes fill the thing with raisins and sultanas, but I don't think they're necessary. The dish is improved immeasurably if the spices are freshly ground, but it's pretty decent even with powdered spice.

Bobotie

Preheat the oven to fan 160°C/325°F/Gas 4. Heat the oil in a deep, heavy, 2.5–3-litre/4½–5-pint casserole (about 23cm/9 inches diameter), add the onions and garlic and cook until soft, about 10 minutes. Stir in the curry powder, cumin, coriander, turmeric and cayenne and cook for a minute or so, until you can smell the spices. Remove from the heat. Add the minced meat, Worcestershire sauce and mango chutney and mix well.

Mix together the bread, milk, lemon rind and juice, egg, bay leaves, salt and pepper. Add to the casserole and mix well. Cover with foil and cook for 1 hour.

Turn up the oven to fan 180°C/350°F/Gas 6. To make the topping, mix together the milk, eggs and a pinch of salt. Pour over the meat and cook, uncovered, for another 20–25 minutes, until set and pale golden. Serve with rice.

SERVES 4

1 tbsp groundnut or vegetable oil
2 large onions, finely chopped
2 garlic cloves, finely chopped
1 tbsp good curry powder
½ tsp cumin seeds, toasted until fragrant, then ground in a mortar and pestle
½ tsp coriander seeds, toasted until fragrant, then ground in a mortar and pestle
¼ tsp ground turmeric
¼ tsp cayenne pepper
450g/1lb minced beef or lamb
1 tbsp Worcestershire sauce
2 tbsp mango chutney
2 slices of day-old white bread, crusts removed, torn into small pieces
5 tbsp full-fat milk
4 strips of unwaxed lemon rind and the juice of 1 lemon
1 large egg, beaten
4 bay leaves
sea salt and freshly ground black pepper
boiled basmati rice, to serve

TOPPING
250ml/9fl oz whole milk
2 large eggs

'The queen of all sauces — our beloved, immortal and mouth-watering ragù.' Nello Oliviero, Neapolitan gastronome.

Ah, Naples. Considered by many as filthy, dirty and dangerous, a southern Italian wretch who has seen better days. But for me it's Italy's greatest city, endlessly invaded and occupied, but endlessly sexy, thrilling and beautiful. It's also home to the best cooking in the country, as well as two of my favourite restaurants in the world (Da Dora for fish and Da Michele for pizza). This is still a poor area of the country, and meat doesn't play a huge role in its traditional cookery. But this slow-cooked ragù is a masterpiece, the pride of every Sunday lunch, simmered and devoured with love and lust. 'You must stay with it, guide it, caress it for hours,' writes Jeanne Carola Francesconi in La Cucina Napoletana, *'so that the aromas of its various components can be released and mingle with each other.' This isn't mere tomato sauce, rather Neapolitan lifeblood. I've adapted this recipe from Arthur Schwartz's magnificent* Naples at Table. *It tastes even better after reading* Naples '44, *Norman Lewis's masterpiece on this most magical and seductive of cities.*

Neapolitan Ragù

SERVES 6–8

1–2 tbsp extra virgin olive oil

250g/9oz rindless pork belly, cut into large chunks

250g/9oz stewing veal

250g/9oz beef shin, cut into chunks

2 onions, finely chopped

½ bottle (37.5cl) of punchy red wine

3 x 400g/14oz cans of chopped tomatoes

big pinch of sea salt

big pinch of dried chilli flakes

handful of fresh parsley, finely chopped

Heat 1 tbsp oil in a large heavy pot over a medium–high heat and brown all the meat, in separate batches, until well browned – around 5 minutes for each batch. Start with the pork belly as it will release some fat, but add more oil if the meat starts to stick.

After removing the final batch of meat, tip the onions into the pan and cook over a low heat for about 10 minutes, until soft, stirring and scraping up the crisped bits of meat stuck on the bottom of the pan.

Return all the meat to the pan, add the wine and reduce over a high heat.

Add the tomatoes, salt and chilli and simmer very gently for 3–4 hours. Stir every 15 minutes or so, skimming off any excess fat. You may need to add a little water, 100ml/3½fl oz at a time, if the sauce begins to stick in the last couple of hours.

The Neapolitans would remove the meat and serve the sauce with pasta to start, then serve the meat separately for a next course. But I like it all together. Scatter on the parsley and serve with a pile of cooked fusilli or spaghetti.

Smoky pork, soft noodles and fistfuls of cool herbs … bun cha is seriously elegant street food, a northern Vietnamese classic. Sadly, even in this internet-enlightened age, some of the more obscure herbs are impossible to find. Still, this is a dish of glorious contrasts, subtle and seductive.

Bun Cha

Mix the fish sauce, soy sauce, spring onions, shallots and garlic in a bowl. Add the pork, cover and marinate in the fridge for at least 3 hours or, better still, overnight.

Light your barbecue and wait until the coals are white-hot, or heat your griddle pan until it's smoking hot.

Cook the noodles according to the packet instructions, rinse with cold water, then drain.

To make the dressing, mix all the ingredients in a pan and heat until the sugar has dissolved; set aside.

Drain the pork and grill over a very high heat until charred and burnished – around 5 minutes, until cooked through, turning twice.

Mix the noodles with the bean sprouts in a large bowl. Add the herbs, lettuce, pork and 2 tbsp of the dressing and toss together. Divide among four bowls, pour over the remaining dressing and serve.

SERVES 4

4 tbsp fish sauce

4 tbsp dark soy sauce

6 spring onions, sliced diagonally

4 Thai (or 1 banana) shallots, sliced

3 garlic cloves, crushed

500g/1lb 2oz rindless pork belly, thinly sliced

225g/8oz dried thin rice noodles

250g/9oz bean sprouts, rinsed

handful of holy basil leaves

handful of mint leaves (Vietnamese if possible)

handful of fresh coriander leaves

1 romaine lettuce, thickly shredded

DRESSING

3 tbsp fish sauce

3 tbsp rice vinegar or white wine vinegar

2 tbsp caster sugar

1 red finger chilli, finely chopped

1 garlic clove, crushed

2 tbsp lime juice

STREET meat

To find the real soul of any culinary culture, the true essence of eating, you have to hit the street. Because it's here, among the fag smoke and diesel fumes, the scent of charcoal and stink of rotting rubbish, where you'll find the finest food of all. From Mexico to Malaysia, Thailand to Taiwan, the secret to good tucker is to get out and pound that pavement.

Street food has little time for prissy garnishes or over-inflated egos. This is all about gutsy, honest dishes, with the rough edges left very much intact. It's gloriously democratic too, the great edible leveller. I've seen stretch limousines beside Guadalajaran taco stands, and bodyguards lurking by Beijing noodle stalls. There's no place for snobbery here. Yet just because it's cheap and quick doesn't mean street food lacks elegance or art. The soft tangle of noodles, that verdant crunch of herbs, all mixed with smoky pork, makes Vietnamese bun cha (*see* page 79) a magnificent mouthful. And few things can beat that first hot, salty bite of *panelle* (*see* page 211), made fresh on the Palermo streets. Instant, joyous gratification.

The best street food, for me, is to be found on the byways and back roads of Mexico and Thailand. Give me tacos al carbon (*see* page 16) loaded with fresh salsa and charred spring onions, proper grilled satay (*see* pages 18 and 62) and charred lamb skewers (*see* page 52). But India, Laos, Malaysia, Singapore, China and Lebanon have their own thriving and delectable street feasts, too. Even Britain, a country whose most recent contribution to the canon of pavement feasting is the 'donkey cock' hotdog, once had a thriving street food culture, with vendors flogging everything from cold fried fish and eel pies to pickled sheep's feet and baked spuds. They've long since disappeared, but recently, at places like Kerb in King's Cross, and Whitecross Street Market, the hungry pedestrian has been able to find all manner of edible pleasure, from kimchi sliders and venison burgers to lovely Luardos burritos.

Some of the greatest things to have ever passed my lips have been born on the street. Two different falafel sandwiches from two stalls, bang next door to each other, owned by two brothers who fell out years back. And despite being less than a metre apart, they never exchange a word. Or a noodle soup – bought from little more than a hut just outside Luang Prabang in Laos – so silken and fragrant that I can still taste its beefy heft.

One of the main tenets of good street food is that everything is made in large amounts. I've had to scale down the recipes, but I don't think they suffer. Of course, these are not strictly authentic ('Authenticity in cuisine is a will-o'-the-wisp, elusive and impossible to define – or, rather, all too easy to define, except that everyone defines it differently,' in the words of food writer Colman Andrews), as you're going to be cooking in your kitchen, rather than over glowing embers or flickering propane flame. They'll never taste as they would on a sultry, steamy Bangkok night. Or in the frantic, cacophonous bustle of a Delhi bazaar. But I haven't rubbed off any rough edges. Because it's the rough edges that make good street food so thrilling, addictive and downright sublime.

Forget all those penny-pinching also-rans, with their mean slices of slimy ham and sparse sprinkling of cheese. This fried sandwich is about generosity and oozing allure. This isn't a classic Croque Monsieur as it lacks béchamel sauce poured all over the top. Too much hassle by far. Anyway, dipping the bread in egg gives a similar sort of result. The bread must be white, preferably a posh or homemade loaf. But I'll never hear a word against the cheap white stuff either. Crusts must be removed. And it must be fried in butter.

Mr Croque

SERVES 2

Dijon mustard

4 slices of white bread, crusts
   removed

2 thickish slices of good ham,
   any gristle removed

75g/2¾oz Gruyère cheese,
   finely grated

2 large eggs, beaten

25g/1oz butter

green salad, to serve

Spread a decent layer of mustard on one side of each slice of bread. Then add the ham and cheese to two of the slices and place the other slices of bread on top.

Pour the eggs into a shallow dish and dip each sandwich in them, turning carefully to coat both sides.

Melt the butter in a large non-stick frying pan over a medium heat until it starts to foam. Cook the sandwiches until golden, about 5–6 minutes, turning halfway through. Serve with a crisp green salad.

Named after those dashing Mexican horsemen, or charros, *these beans are cooked with tomatoes, chilli and pork in some form or other. I use chorizo, but feel free to use salt pork, bacon or any other kind of cured pork.*

Frijoles a la Charra

If you are using soaked dried beans, drain and rinse them, then put them in a pan with water to cover, bring to the boil and simmer for 45 minutes–1 hour, until tender. Drain and set aside.

Heat the oil in a wide, heavy pan and fry the chorizo for a minute or so until the oils start to release, then add the onions and garlic and cook for about 10 minutes, until soft.

Add the jalapeño and chipotle chillies and cook for another 2 minutes. Add the vinegar and cook for a minute or so, until the liquid has disappeared.

Add the beans, tomatoes, bay leaf and 500ml/18fl oz water and simmer for about 25 minutes. Season to taste. Serve with tortillas.

SERVES 4

250g/9oz dried pinto beans, soaked in cold water overnight, or 2 x 400g/14oz cans, rinsed and drained

1 tbsp olive oil

about 150g/5½oz cooking chorizo, cut into 1cm/½-inch pieces

2 onions, roughly chopped

2 garlic cloves, chopped

2 fresh jalapeño or long green chillies, chopped

3 chipotle chillies, soaked in just-boiled water for 20 minutes, drained and chopped

2 tbsp white wine vinegar

400g/14oz can of chopped tomatoes

1 bay leaf

sea salt

tortillas, to serve

A trip to a Laotian country market can be a sobering experience. Beautiful jungle cats, with their thick fur, sit on stalls, curled up as if asleep. But they're dead, and ready for the pot. Along with various dried rats, frogs, snakes and tiny jungle birds. This isn't extreme eating though, rather base survival. Laos is a poor, mainly rural, country and nothing edible is taken for granted. This dish, though, is rather more acceptable to Western palates, bulking out a small amount of minced pork with aubergine and spring onions.

Fried Aubergine with Pork

SERVES 2

4 tbsp groundnut or sunflower oil

2 aubergines, cut into 2cm/¾-inch chunks

4 garlic cloves, finely chopped

125g/4½oz minced pork

big pinch of sugar

big pinch of salt

4 tbsp oyster sauce

5 spring onions, sliced diagonally into 2cm/¾-inch pieces

steamed sticky rice, to serve

Heat 3 tbsp oil in a wok or frying pan, add the aubergines and cook over a high heat for around 5–6 minutes, until they are soft and starting to turn golden. Remove with a slotted spoon and set aside.

Reduce the heat to medium, add a little more oil if need be, then add the garlic. When it starts to turn golden, add the pork and stir-fry until cooked. Add the sugar, salt and oyster sauce, then whack up the heat. Add the aubergines and spring onions and stir-fry for 1–2 minutes. Serve hot, with sticky rice.

The Tuscans were once known as mangiafagioli, *or 'bean eaters', by other Italians, thanks to their appetite for* 'la carne dei poveri', *the lowly white cannellini bean. They knew how to stretch things out. Although those parsimonious locals were probably scared off years back by the fleets of British bankers and barristers who made the area their own, chugging super-Tuscans and trotting off every morning to pick up their copies of the* Daily Mail *and* Financial Times. *Dried beans, soaked overnight before cooking, have a better consistency, but this is a store-cupboard dish and canned beans will do fine. I use onion in my version, which is deeply inauthentic. But 'authenticity' is a much overused word.*

Tuscan-ish Sausage and Bean Stew

SERVES 4

125g/4½oz dried cannellini beans, soaked in cold water overnight, or 1 x 400g/14oz can, rinsed and drained
1 bay leaf (if using dried beans)
4 black peppercorns (if using dried beans)
4 garlic cloves
salt
1 tbsp olive oil
1 onion, finely chopped
6 fresh Italian sausages (or the best, most meaty, British ones you can find)
2 x 400g/14oz cans of chopped tomatoes
pinch of dried chilli flakes
crusty bread, to serve

If you are using soaked dried beans, drain and rinse them, then put them in a pan with the bay leaf, peppercorns, one whole peeled garlic clove, and cold water to cover. Bring to the boil for 10 minutes, then reduce the heat and simmer gently for 1½–2 hours, until soft but not breaking apart. Add a pinch of salt towards the end of the cooking time. Drain the beans, reserving about 175ml/6fl oz of the cooking liquor.

Finely chop the remaining garlic. Heat the oil in a large frying pan, add the onion and chopped garlic and soften for 5 minutes. Slice the sausages and squeeze the meat into the pan, then cook over a medium–high heat, breaking up the meat with a wooden spoon, until lightly browned.

Add the tomatoes and chilli, along with the bean liquor (or 175ml/6fl oz water if using canned beans), and simmer for 15 minutes. Add the beans and cook for 15 minutes more, until the sauce is good and thick. Try not to squash the beans too much, keeping them in one piece. Serve with crusty bread.

This is the classic, 'pure' version of one of my favourite pasta sauces, and rather more pared back than the recipe I gave in Let's Eat, *which was inspired by* The River Café Cook Book *by Rose Gray and Ruth Rogers. I first tried the real thing (if there is such a thing) in a cramped trattoria, called Cucina di Enzo, in Rome. I was with Jacob Kenedy, brilliant chef and owner of London restaurant Bocca di Lupo, and he was showing me Roman food like I've never seen before. The Romans like their food robust. As Jacob pointed out, between bites, 'There's nothing fine or fancy here, and things can be, well, kind of brutal.' There are lots of very strong flavours, be it pork, or pecorino, or pepper. 'And these flavours are turned right up to the max. Subtle, it ain't.' After mountains of* carciofi alla giudea *(artichokes fried in olive oil) and vast plates of tripe stewed in tomato, we dug into spaghetti all'Amatriciana, made with* guanciale *(cured pig's cheek) and that other great Roman staple, pecorino. It's big and bold and beautifully Roman.*

Real Roman Spaghetti all'Amatriciana

Heat a glug of oil in a frying pan, add the chilli and cook for 30 seconds. Add the *guanciale* and fry until crisp. Add the tomatoes and cook for 10–15 minutes, until the sauce starts to thicken.

Meanwhile, cook the pasta in boiling water until al dente. Drain and add to the sauce, then throw in the pecorino, lots of black pepper and a little salt to taste. Serve immediately, with extra pecorino.

SERVES 4

olive oil
big pinch of dried chilli flakes
250g/9oz *guanciale* or
    pancetta, cut into strips
400g/14oz can of chopped
    tomatoes
500g/1lb 2oz spaghetti or
    bucatini
150g/5½oz pecorino cheese,
    grated, plus extra to serve
sea salt and freshly ground
    black pepper

Ham, eggs and fried potatoes. In one glorious dish. A little green or red chilli adds its fiery magic too.

Baked Eggs with Ham and Spicy Potatoes

SERVES 4

about 10 small new potatoes, or any waxy variety, cut into 5mm/¼-inch thick slices
sea salt and freshly ground black pepper
4 tbsp olive oil
3 green or red finger chillies, chopped
1 garlic clove, thinly sliced
about 6 thick slices of good British ham, torn in half
4 large eggs
bread, to serve

Put the potatoes in a pan of salted water, bring to the boil and simmer for 10 minutes, until cooked but still firm. Drain in a colander. Preheat the oven to fan 200°C/400°F/Gas 7.

Pour 2 tbsp oil into a frying pan, add the chillies and garlic and cook over a low heat until soft. Using a slotted spoon, remove the chillies and garlic and set aside. Add another 1 tbsp oil, whack up the heat and fry the potatoes until burnished and crisp. Return the chillies and garlic to the pan, mix and remove from the heat.

Oil four heatproof bowls (ramekins are a little small; the best are those earthenware tapas bowls). Line each bowl with ham and potatoes, leaving a dip for the eggs. Place the bowls on a baking tray and bake for 5 minutes.

Take the tray out of the oven, crack an egg into each dish, season, and return to the oven for 10 minutes, or until the whites are just firm and the yolks just runny. Serve with good bread for mopping up the juices.

The superstar of Southern black-eyed pea dishes (and believe me, there's an entire constellation out there), this is traditionally eaten on New Year's Day, for good luck and prosperity. Cornbread and collard greens are the almost compulsory accompaniments, collard greens being members of the Brassica family, close cousins of cabbage. As to the name... there are endless variations on the story of John hoppin' with joy when his wife took the dish out of the oven, or children hoppin' around the tables in greedy anticipation of the dish to come. Etymologists have a rather more sober slant: that it's a corruption of pois au pigeon, *the pigeon pea being another bean brought from Africa into America. Food historians see it as a West Indian dish, introduced by slaves. Ham hocks are easily available at the butcher, and cheap too. If the ham is really salty, soak overnight in cold water before cooking.*

Hoppin' John

Put the ham hock in a pan with the bay leaves, add cold water to cover and bring to the boil, then cover with a lid and simmer for about 1 hour.

Add the onions, celery, chilli flakes, dried whole chilli and peppercorns and simmer for 30 minutes.

Add the beans and boil for 10 minutes, then reduce the heat and simmer for a further 20–30 minutes, until the ham is cooked. You don't want mushy peas, rather a good firmness and bite.

Meanwhile, 20 minutes before the beans are done, cook the rice in lightly salted boiling water, then drain.

Drain any remaining liquid from the ham mixture. Break up the ham and mix it into the beans. Stir in the rice, and season to taste. Add the tomatoes and parsley. Serve with cornbread and collard greens. Douse very liberally with hot sauce.

SERVES 6

1 uncooked ham hock (about 1kg/2lb 4oz)

2 bay leaves

3 onions, roughly chopped

6 celery stalks, with leaves, diced

1 tsp dried chilli flakes

1 dried red chilli

4 black peppercorns

250g/9oz black-eyed peas, soaked in cold water overnight, drained

200g/7oz basmati rice

sea salt and freshly ground black pepper

3 tomatoes, deseeded and diced

handful of fresh parsley, roughly chopped

Jalapeño Cornbread (*see* page 147), to serve

collard greens, blanched, to serve

hot sauce, such as Tabasco, to serve

This soupy stew has various incarnations all over the Iberian peninsula. Actually, the classic combination of tiny scraps of meat with lots of stodgy, cheap beans is found all over the world. If you can lay your hands on a cooked ham bone, then so much the better. Otherwise, go for ham hocks and a couple of chorizos. As is so often the case, this dish tastes better after a day's rest.

Andalucian Chickpea Stew (Potaje de garbanzos)

Put the ham hock, chorizo and ham bone, if using, in a very large pan with around 4 litres/7 pints cold water. Bring to the boil, skim, then add the bay leaf and a glug of olive oil. Reduce the heat and simmer for 1½–2 hours, or until tender.

Drain and rinse the dried chickpeas, if using, and add them to the pan. Bring back to the boil, then simmer for another 40 minutes–1 hour, until just tender (simmer without the chickpeas if using canned).

Heat a glug of olive oil in a frying pan and cook the garlic until soft. Remove with a slotted spoon and set aside, add the bread and fry gently until crisp. Sprinkle over the parsley.

Add the bread, parsley and garlic to the soup, along with the spinach, potatoes and tomatoes. Cook for 20 minutes, adding the canned chickpeas, if using, after about 10 minutes, until the chickpeas are soft but not mushy. Break up and stir in the ham, remove the bone, if using, and season with salt and pepper to taste. Serve hot.

SERVES 6

1 uncooked ham hock (about 1kg/2lb 4oz), soaked in cold water overnight in the fridge, drained

200g/7oz cooking chorizo, sliced

1 cooked ham bone (optional)

1 bay leaf

2–3 tbsp olive oil

250g/9oz dried chickpeas, soaked in cold water overnight, or 2 x 400g/14oz cans, rinsed and drained

4 garlic cloves, sliced

50g/1¾oz good white rustic bread, torn into pieces

400g/14oz spinach (not baby spinach) or kale, trimmed and roughly chopped

250g/9oz floury potatoes, peeled and cut into small dice

2 tomatoes, chopped

sea salt and freshly ground black pepper

You'll find this dish – Feijoada – all over Portugal. Indeed, you'll find mixes of cured pork and beans all over the Iberian peninsula. Cheap, cheerful and just the right side of stodge, it can be made with canned beans, but soaked dried beans do have a better bite.

Portuguese Bean Stew

SERVES 4

250g/9oz dried butter beans, soaked in cold water overnight, or 2 x 400g/14oz cans, rinsed and drained
2 onions
150g/5½oz streaky bacon, cut into 2cm/¾-inch pieces
200g/7oz cooking chorizo, cut into 1.5cm/⅝-inch pieces
good dash of sherry vinegar
1 garlic clove, sliced
2 tomatoes, peeled, deseeded and chopped
1 bay leaf
sea salt and freshly ground black pepper
handful of fresh parsley, roughly chopped

If you are using soaked dried beans, drain and rinse them, then put them in a pan with a whole peeled onion. Add cold water to cover and bring to the boil for 10 minutes, then simmer until tender, about 1½–2 hours. Drain and keep the liquor.

Thinly slice the remaining onion. Heat a large non-stick frying pan and cook the bacon and chorizo until lightly browned. Remove and set aside. Deglaze the pan with the vinegar, then add the remaining onion and the garlic and cook for 10 minutes, until soft.

Add the tomatoes and bay leaf and return the cooked meat to the pan, along with 5–6 tbsp of the reserved bean liquor, or 100ml/3½fl oz cold water if using canned beans, and cook for 2 minutes over a high heat. Add the beans, season to taste, and cook for a few minutes, until hot. Sprinkle over the parsley and serve.

Hogget is simply lamb with wanderlust and a decent education. It's killed when it's between twelve and eighteen months old, so it knows a thing or two about flavour. It doesn't overwhelm, like old mutton, yet still bleats with ovine delight. As for puddings, they're one of those rare culinary arts, along with roasting and stewing, at which the British excel. You want suet pastry to be rich but not too dry, soft but strong enough to hold in its blessed contents.

Hogget Pudding

MAKES 6

3 tbsp sunflower oil

700g/1lb 9oz boneless shoulder of hogget, trimmed of excess fat and cut into 3cm/1¼-inch chunks

2 onions, roughly chopped

1 large carrot, roughly chopped

1 leek, sliced

1 celery stalk, diced

2 garlic cloves, chopped

1 tbsp plain flour

250ml/9fl oz Madeira or red wine

500ml/18fl oz fresh hot lamb stock (use chicken if you can't get it)

1 tbsp redcurrant jelly

2 bay leaves

5 black peppercorns

big pinch of chopped fresh parsley

little butter for greasing

sea salt and freshly ground black pepper

peas, to serve

SUET CRUST

350g/12oz self-raising flour, sifted

175g/6oz shredded beef suet

1 tsp salt

Preheat the oven to fan 150°C/300°F/Gas 3. Slosh 2 tbsp oil into a heavy pan over a high heat. Brown the meat in batches and set aside. Reduce the heat, add the remaining oil and cook the onions for 10 minutes, until soft. Add the carrot, leek, celery and garlic and cook for 5 minutes. Return the meat to the pan, add the flour, and cook for a minute, stirring. Gradually pour in the Madeira, scraping up any meaty bits. Add the stock, redcurrant jelly, bay and peppercorns. Cover and bake for 1½ hours, until tender. Stir in the parsley, re-cover, and leave to cool for an hour. Remove as much fat as you can.

While the filling is cooking, make the suet crust: mix the self-raising flour, suet and salt in a bowl. Gradually add 250ml/9fl oz cold water, until you have a firm dough. Wrap in clingfilm and chill in the fridge for 1 hour.

Grease six 200ml/7fl oz pudding dishes with butter. Put in the fridge for 20 minutes, then re-butter. Divide the dough into six balls, then reserve one-third from each ball for the lids. Roll out each ball to a circle 14cm/5½ inches across and 5mm/¼ inch thick and line the dishes with the dough, pushing it into the base. Preheat the oven to fan 170°C/340°F/Gas 5.

Spoon the filling into the suet crusts until it almost reaches the top. Brush the rims with water and stick on the lids. Press to seal, then trim with a knife. Cover with baking parchment with a pleat in the middle, then with pleated foil. Secure with string. Repeat for the remaining puddings.

Place the puddings in a roasting tin. Pour just-boiled water into the tin until it comes halfway up the pudding bowls. Cover the tin with foil. Bake for 1½ hours. Holding the bowls with a tea towel, snip the string and peel away the foil and parchment. Tip the puddings onto a plate and serve with peas.

Cottage pie encased in a baked potato shell. Simple, but inspired. Of course, I can't take any credit at all (the idea came from a chef friend, Stuart). Rocket science, this ain't. Use lamb instead of beef if you want to make this a shepherd's, rather than cottage, dish.

Cottage Pie Tots

Preheat the oven to fan 200°C/400°F/Gas 7. Bake the potatoes for about 1 hour, until the skins are crisp and the flesh tender.

Meanwhile, heat the oil in a heavy pan over a medium heat and cook the onions and garlic until soft, about 10 minutes. Turn up the heat, add the minced meat and brown, breaking up the meat with a wooden spoon. Add the tomato purée, stock and Worcestershire sauce. Simmer gently for 30 minutes, until the beef is tender and the sauce is thick, stirring regularly. Leave to cool slightly.

Slice off the tops of the potatoes and scoop out soft potato flesh into a bowl. Mix with the butter, salt and pepper. Preheat the grill to high.

Fill the scooped-out potato skins with the mince mixture, then top with a spoonful of the soft potato. Grill for 2 minutes, until the top is lightly browned. Serve hot.

SERVES 4

4 similarly sized baking
   potatoes, washed and
   sprinkled with sea salt
1 tbsp olive oil
2 onions, finely chopped
3 garlic cloves, finely chopped
500g/1lb 2oz good minced
   beef (or lamb)
2 tbsp tomato purée
750ml/1¼ pints beef stock
   (*see* page 227, or use
   Stockpot, or canned beef
   consommé; Baxters,
   of course)
2 tbsp Worcestershire sauce
40g/1½oz butter
sea salt and freshly ground
   black pepper

While we happily devour steak tartare, we're not so keen when it comes to raw lamb. But some of the best food I have eaten in Beirut and Istanbul has never been near a flame. Lumps of richly quivering lamb's liver, raw and gleaming, dipped in za'atar. And kibbeh nayyeh, lamb pounded with bulgur wheat and onion, eaten with a mass of billowing pitta bread. The lamb must be the best you can find, and either ground by the butcher or at home. It's traditionally pounded in a pestle and mortar, and pundits argue that this gives a finer texture. I use the food processor. Pre-packed minced lamb has many uses, but making kibbeh nayyeh is certainly not one of them.

Kibbeh Nayyeh

SERVES 4–6

125g/4½oz bulgur wheat
500g/1lb 2oz lean leg of lamb,
    trimmed of fat and sinew,
    cut into cubes
4–6 ice cubes
1 large onion, roughly
    chopped
2 tsp cumin seeds, toasted until
    fragrant, then ground in a
    mortar and pestle
¼ tsp ground cinnamon
sea salt and freshly ground
    black pepper
a big glug of olive oil
juice of ½ lemon (optional)
handful of fresh mint, roughly
    chopped
handful of fresh parsley,
    roughly chopped
3 spring onions, roughly
    chopped

TO SERVE
hot pitta breads (*see* page 212)
1 romaine lettuce, broken into
    leaves
pickled chillies
1 white onion, roughly
    chopped
radishes

Cook the bulgur wheat in boiling water for 8–10 minutes, until just tender. Drain in a sieve, then rinse under running water until cold. Soak in cold water for 20 minutes, then drain and squeeze out excess water.

In a food processor, blitz the lamb with the ice, onion, cumin, cinnamon and a pinch of salt and pepper until you have a thick paste.

Mix the lamb with the bulgur, spread onto a dish and anoint with olive oil and a squeeze of lemon juice if you like, then garnish with mint, parsley and spring onions.

Shape into fat, finger-sized patties. Serve with hot pitta breads and cool romaine lettuce leaves, pickled chillies, chopped white onion and radishes on the side.

Stuff turkey. Seriously, I've never understood why perfectly civilised people lose all vestige of common sense once a year and start gibbering about turkey. I'd far rather eat a great roast rib of beef. Or a brace of proper chickens. Anything rather than this gobbling American arriviste. But hey ho, I'm in the minority. So if you are faced with acres of leftover festive flesh, this makes everything seem a whole lot more bearable.

Turkey Hash

Heat 2 tbsp oil in a frying pan over a medium heat, then cook the onion and chillies for about 10 minutes, until soft. Set aside and leave to cool.

Fry the bacon until crisp, then crumble it.

Tip the onion, chillies and bacon into a bowl, then add the turkey, potatoes, egg, parsley and hot sauce. Season generously, then form into eight patties.

Heat half the butter with 1 tbsp oil in a large frying pan over a medium heat and cook the patties, in two batches, for 2½–3 minutes on each side, until crisp and golden; add the remaining butter and oil to cook the second batch. Serve hot, topped with a poached egg.

SERVES 4

4 tbsp olive oil
1 large onion, chopped
2–4 jalapeño or green finger
   chillies, finely chopped
4 rashers of streaky bacon
350g/12oz cold cooked turkey,
   roughly chopped
4 leftover cold roast potatoes,
   roughly smashed, or 2 big
   cooked floury potatoes,
   roughly mashed
1 egg, lightly beaten
handful of fresh parsley,
   roughly chopped
1 tsp hot sauce, such as
   Tabasco
sea salt and freshly ground
   black pepper
40g/1½oz butter
4 soft poached eggs, to serve

new vs

WORLD

OLD

WORLD

Imagine America without fried chicken, bacon, burgers and hotdogs, Mexico without carnitas, or Argentina bereft of fat slabs of intricately marbled steak. These dishes are so intrinsically bound up in the edible history of each country that they seem to have been there from the year dot. Yet it was a mere 500 years ago that the pig came trotting into the New World, carried, oinking and squealing, on shore by the invading Spanish armies.

So for Ponce de León and Pedro de Alvarado, those gold-hungry invaders, it wasn't all mere rape and pillage. They were both responsible for the introduction of the pig to the New World. Take gold, and lives, give pig. Hardly a fair trade, but at least something positive came out of all that plundering. Oh, and another big shout out to Francisco Vásquez de Coronado who, when not seeking illicit fortune, managed to bring cattle to the North American South West, turning Pueblo hunters into cattle folk. And laying the foundation for the entire modern US beef industry.

But it was the Colombian Exchange (named after Christopher 'The Big Man' Columbus, following his sojourn in 1492) that turned out to be one of the most important events in the history of world food. Not only were pigs and cattle introduced from Old World to New, but sheep, goats (excluding the indigenous mountain varieties), chickens (although there is archaeological evidence of pre-Colombian chickens), horses, mules, domestic cats and dogs too. Plus a devastating dose of smallpox, yellow fever, common cold, bubonic plague, malaria and measles.

It wasn't all one way. In exchange for this veritable feast of flesh, the Old World got potatoes, maize, chillies, tomatoes, grapes, cotton, cocoa and, erm, the bell pepper. Bloody bell peppers. Thanks for that one, Chris. Oh, and syphilis, the gift that just keeps on giving. The animals, though, were a little less gustatorially exciting. Turkeys, guinea pigs and llama. Nice. If you run a petting zoo.

As to the roots of all these beloved edible animals, look east. To Central Asia, southern Turkey and Iran. Where, along with domesticated wheat and barley, long-haired mouflon sheep were kept for their meat, in Mesopotamia, around 9000BC. Goats were domesticated earlier still, from the wild *Capra aegagrus*, by Neolithic farmers as far back as 11,000BC, in the Euphrates river valley in Turkey, and the Zagros mountains of Iraq.

Domesticated chickens were descended from the wild red jungle fowl of South and Southeast Asia, about 8000 years ago. And in China, around 5400BC. Cattle were domesticated twice, if not three times: once around 10,500BC, in the pre-pottery Neolithic cultures in the Taurus mountains; and in the valleys of the Tigris and Euphrates rivers; and again in the Indus valley of India. Central and South Asia seems to be the crux of all the meat we love to eat.

Swine, though, are more of an enigma. Wild pigs are indigenous to Europe, but there's also evidence that pigs were domesticated in Central Asia in around 9000BC. And like goats, sheep, chickens and cattle, they were brought into Europe, 7000 years back, by Central Asian people. Phew. Well, that's the history part over. Now, back to the eating.

Ah, the kebab, the late-night last resort of the peckish toper. B.O.-scented flaps of flesh forced into a stale pitta with radioactive chilli sauce. Yuck! But a good kebab is something wonderful. This recipe came about when my wife asked for a healthy-ish dish for dinner. Wandering down the Uxbridge Road on my way home, I found fresh flatbread. And endless spices. This has a kick and zing, but nothing too overwhelming. The za'atar adds that scent of Eastern promise.

Harissa and Za'atar Marinated Chicken Kebab with Chilli Raita

MAKES 4

6 skinless, boneless
  chicken thighs, cut into
  2.5cm/1-inch chunks
juice of 1 small lemon
1 tbsp harissa paste
1 tbsp za'atar
1 tbsp olive oil
4 flatbreads or large pitta
  breads (*see* page 212)
1 head of round lettuce,
  chopped
handful of fresh coriander
  leaves, roughly chopped
handful of fresh parsley,
  roughly chopped

TOMATO AND ONION SALAD
2 tomatoes, roughly chopped
1 red onion, roughly chopped
2 bird's-eye chillies, chopped
½ cucumber, deseeded and
  finely chopped
1 tbsp white wine vinegar
big pinch of sea salt

CHILLI RAITA
200g/7oz natural yogurt
½ cucumber, deseeded and
  finely chopped
1 green finger chilli, finely
  chopped

Mix the chicken with the lemon juice, harissa and za'atar. Cover and marinate in the fridge for at least 1 hour, or longer if possible.

To make the salad, mix all the ingredients together and leave to sit for 10 minutes.

Mix together the ingredients for the raita, add a pinch of salt and leave to sit.

Drain the chicken well. Heat the oil in a non-stick pan or griddle pan and cook the chicken for 3 minutes on each side, until cooked through, with piping-hot juices that have no sign of pink when the largest piece is cut in half.

Heat the breads. Smear chilli raita all over, then the lettuce and salad. Top with chicken pieces and herbs, and wrap.

Chicken salad, eh? Too often an edible after-thought, little more than a few desultory cubes of bone-dry chicken, cowering under a couple of limp lettuce leaves. And if you're really unlucky, you might stumble across a few chunks of raw pepper. Really, what is the point of raw peppers? In the United States, and New York in particular, they do it properly. Usually in the form of the Cobb salad, big and unashamedly bounteous. Created by one Robert Cobb in 1936 at the Brown Derby in Hollywood, the key is a sharp dressing ('be mindful that chicken salad is only as good as the amount and quality of the dressing used to bind the ingredients,' warns food scribe James Villas in Stalking the Green Fairy, *'… a dry salad is virtually inedible; one that is overdressed can be appalling'), plus perfectly poached chicken. There's even, would you believe it, a mnemonic for Cobb salad – EAT COBB: Egg, Avocado, Tomato, Chicken, Onion, Bacon, Blue cheese. Just in case you forget the ingredients.*

Cobb Salad

SERVES 6

2 skinless chicken breasts
6 black peppercorns
1 bay leaf
1 celery stalk, split
½ onion
6 strips of smoked streaky
    bacon
bunch of watercress, thick
    stems removed
1 head of chicory, separated
1 large head of romaine
    lettuce, separated
4 hard-boiled eggs, chopped
1 avocado, chopped
4 tomatoes, chopped
100g/3½oz Roquefort or other
    well-behaved blue cheese,
    diced or crumbled

DRESSING
3 tbsp white wine vinegar
fine sea salt and freshly
    ground black pepper
big pinch of mustard powder
½ tsp caster sugar
jig of Worcestershire sauce
150ml/5fl oz extra virgin
    olive oil

Put the chicken in a pan with the peppercorns, bay leaf, celery and onion and water to cover. Bring to the boil, reduce the heat to a mere 'blip, blip', cover and poach for 15 minutes, until the chicken is piping hot and cooked through, with no sign of pink in the juices when the thickest part is pierced with a skewer. Transfer the chicken to a plate and leave to cool.

Fry the bacon until cooked, then roughly chop it and set aside.

Cut the chicken meat into 2.5cm/1-inch cubes and put in a large bowl. Add the bacon, watercress, chicory, romaine lettuce, eggs, avocado, tomatoes and cheese, and toss.

Make the dressing by whisking together the vinegar, salt, pepper, mustard powder, sugar and Worcestershire sauce. When combined, whisk in the oil. Taste for seasoning, then dribble over the salad so every leaf is gleaming with it, but not drenched.

This is a Thai curry that doesn't use coconut milk, so there's little respite from the chilli heat. I tried it in the market at Samut Sakhon, south-west of Bangkok, where they made it with quail. It renders all conversation pretty impossible for a few minutes, but it has other, more subtle qualities too. You just have to wait for your mouth to calm down before you appreciate them. If you can be bothered to mince quail, then great. But chicken's fine. I've adapted this from a recipe by David Thompson. Because as Carly Simon once sang, nobody does it better.

Chicken Jungle Curry

To make the spice paste, blitz all the ingredients in a small blender. If it is too thick, add a little water – no more than 2–3 tbsp. Halfway through, stop and scrape the sides of the blender with a spatula. Or you could use a pestle and mortar.

Heat the oil in a frying pan or wok and cook the spice paste until fragrant, 'stirring furiously,' as David Thompson says, to stop it sticking. This should be done in a well-ventilated area, or with the extractor on full. When the chilli makes you sneeze, after 2–3 minutes, add the minced chicken and stir-fry over a medium heat for about 3 minutes, or until cooked through. Add the fish sauce and stock and bring to the boil. Mix in the holy basil. Serve with steamed rice.

SERVES 4

1 tsp vegetable oil
3 chicken breasts (400g/14oz), minced
1 tbsp fish sauce
250ml/9fl oz fresh light chicken stock (*see* page 223)
big handful of holy basil leaves
steamed rice, to serve

SPICE PASTE

1 dried long red chilli, deseeded and soaked in just-boiled water for 15 minutes, drained
4 dried bird's-eye chillies
4 fresh red bird's-eye chillies, stalks removed, roughly chopped
big pinch of salt
20g/¾oz fresh galangal, peeled and chopped
2 lemongrass stalks, chopped
4 garlic cloves, chopped
2 tsp Thai shrimp paste

I first tasted this punchy Pakistani curry not on the charcoal-scented streets of Lahore, but in the rather less visceral environs of a Mayfair basement. Hardly the place, I hear you say, to cook up an old-fashioned brow-beader. But the restaurant was Benares and the chef Atul Kochhar, one of the true masters of spice. His version, thrown together with almost raffish insouciance, not only seduced the taste buds, but had them begging for his hand in marriage too. My version is a little less refined, but this is a curry of meaty magnificence.

Chicken Lahori

SERVES 4

4 tbsp vegetable oil
2 black cardamom pods
4 green cardamom pods
1 tsp cumin seeds
2 bay leaves
4 onions, roughly chopped
3 garlic cloves, very finely chopped
3 slices of fresh ginger, peeled and very finely chopped
3 tsp red chilli powder
1½ tbsp ground coriander
½ tsp ground turmeric
4–8 green finger chillies, chopped
5–6 tomatoes, chopped
8 skinless, boneless chicken thighs
2 tbsp natural yogurt
500ml/18fl oz fresh light chicken stock (*see* page 223) or water
pinch of salt
handful of fresh coriander leaves, roughly chopped
1 tsp garam masala (*see* page 222)
steamed or boiled basmati rice, to serve

Heat the oil in a large pan or wok and sauté the whole spices and bay leaves until they crackle and pop. Add the onions and cook for 15 minutes, until lightly browned, then add the garlic and ginger and cook for 1 minute.

Add the red chilli powder, ground coriander, ground turmeric, green chillies and tomatoes and cook for another 5 minutes.

Add the chicken, yogurt, stock and salt. Simmer for 20–25 minutes, until the chicken is piping hot and cooked through, with no sign of pink in the juices when the thickest part is pierced with a skewer. Stir in the coriander and garam masala, and serve with basmati rice.

The average British Thai chicken curry has all the appeal of four-day-old despair. Cloying, oversweet and utterly without charm, it's little wonder that this great dish has fallen so far. But using a fresh paste and coconut milk turns a turgid mess into something elegant, fragrant and deeply seductive. There's the warmth of chilli, a subtle sweetness and the tang of all those fresh herbs and spices.

Thai Chicken Curry

SERVES 4

1 tbsp groundnut oil

2 x 400ml/14fl oz cans of unsweetened coconut milk

6 skinless, boneless chicken thighs, halved

1 tbsp fish sauce

4 kaffir lime leaves, finely shredded (I use frozen)

400ml/14fl oz chicken stock (cube is fine)

175g/6oz baby corn

big handful of fresh Thai basil

steamed jasmine rice, to serve

SPICE PASTE

6–14 bird's-eye chillies, stalks removed

1 tsp sea salt

25g/1oz fresh galangal, peeled and chopped

½ tsp ground turmeric

25g/1oz fresh coriander, stalks chopped, leaves chopped and reserved for garnish

10 Thai (or 2 small banana) shallots, chopped

6 garlic cloves, chopped

2 tsp Thai shrimp paste

10 white peppercorns, ground in a mortar and pestle

1 tsp each cumin and coriander seeds, toasted until fragrant, then ground in a mortar and pestle

Make the spice paste either by pounding everything together in a mortar and pestle, starting with the chillies and salt – authentic, but tiring – or by blitzing the chillies in a food processor, then gradually adding the other ingredients to make a wettish paste. If too dry, add 1–2 tbsp water.

Heat the oil in a large pan and cook the paste over a medium heat for about 1 minute, until all the wonderful aromas begin to fragrance the room. Add the coconut milk and cook for 2 minutes.

Add the chicken, fish sauce, lime leaves and stock and bring to the boil. Reduce the heat and simmer for 15 minutes, until the sauce is reduced and the chicken nearly cooked.

Add the corn and cook for 3 minutes, until the chicken is piping hot and cooked through, with no sign of pink in the juices when you pierce the thickest part with a skewer. Add the basil and cook for another 30 seconds, then turn off the heat and taste. It should be hot, slightly sweet and salty. Scatter with chopped coriander leaves and serve with jasmine rice.

'Parent and child' rice. Not exactly the most sexy of descriptions, although it does have its own, slightly odd, charm. The parent in this case is chicken, the child, yup, you've guessed it, the egg. It's comfort food and should be made with dashi, a staple Japanese stock, which makes all the difference. If you are nowhere near a Japanese shop, chicken stock will do. But it will be a rather different dish.

Oyakodon

Boil the rice until just tender. Crack eggs into a bowl, but do not beat, rather make the mark of Zorro, twice, with chopsticks or a fork.

Meanwhile, put the mirin and sake in a large frying pan and bring to the boil. Add the soy sauce, sugar and dashi, stir well and bring back to the boil.

Add the onion, then spread the mixture out in the pan. Top with the chicken. Bring to the boil, skim, then cover and simmer gently for 10 minutes, until the chicken is cooked through with no sign of pink in the juices when you tear a slice in half.

Pour the egg slowly and evenly over the chicken, shaking the pan. Cook for 30 seconds, then turn off the heat, cover the pan and leave for another 30 seconds.

Drain the rice and divide among four bowls. Pour the soup over the rice and scatter with spring onions.

Dashi stock

Wipe the kombu gently with a damp cloth, but don't wipe away the white residue. Make three slits in the kombu and soak in 500ml/18fl oz cold water for 4–6 hours.

Put the kombu in a pan, add the water and gently bring to the boil, skimming off any scum. Just before it comes to the boil, remove the kombu and turn off the heat.

Add the bonito to the water and bring back to the boil, skimming if needed. Reduce the heat and simmer for 1 minute. Let the bonito flakes sink to the bottom, then strain through a muslin-lined sieve into a bowl; squeeze the muslin to extract the last drops. Cover and keep in the fridge for up to one week.

SERVES 4

100g/3½oz Japanese rice

4 eggs

6 tbsp mirin

2 tbsp sake

4 tbsp dark soy sauce

1 tbsp caster sugar

400ml/14fl oz dashi (see below) or fresh light chicken stock (*see* page 223)

1 onion, thinly sliced

4 skinless, boneless chicken thighs, cut into 2.5cm/1-inch slices

handful of finely chopped spring onions

DASHI STOCK (MAKES 400ML/14FL OZ)

10g/¼oz dried kombu

15g/½oz bonito flakes

I first tried this lime soup in the Yucatan, the Mexican state with the Caribbean coast. We escaped the purpose-built hellhole of Cancún and drove down to Playa del Carmen, which was then – 20 years back – a sleepy coastal town; it's now another sprawling holiday city. I was with an ex-girlfriend and I think we'd had a blazing row. Anyway, this soup seemed to calm things down; it's sharp and fiendishly hot, thanks to a handful of local habanero peppers. One sip, and I'm transported back to those snow-white, sultry beaches.

Sopa di Lima

Pour the oil or lard into a deep frying pan, heat until shimmering, then throw in the tortilla strips and cook for 1–2 minutes, until golden. Remove, drain on kitchen paper and set aside.

Remove all but 2 tbsp of the tortilla-infused oil. Add the onion and cook over a medium heat for 10 minutes, until soft. Add the chillies and garlic, and cook for another 5 minutes. Add the tomatoes, then the stock, salt and chicken. Reduce the heat and simmer for 15–20 minutes, until the chicken is piping hot and cooked through, with no sign of pink in the juices when you pierce the thickest part with a skewer.

Remove the chicken breasts and shred the meat. Return to the soup with the lime juice and slices, and heat until bubbling.

Serve in bowls, topped with the tortilla strips, coriander and sliced avocado.

SERVES 6

200ml/7fl oz groundnut or sunflower oil or lard

6 small corn tortillas (not the soft flour tortillas), cut into thin strips

1 onion, finely chopped

½–2 habanero chillies, finely chopped

2 garlic cloves, very thinly sliced

2 large tomatoes, peeled, deseeded and cut into 1cm/½-inch dice

1.5 litres/2½ pints fresh light chicken stock (*see* page 223)

1½ tsp sea salt flakes

2 skinless, boneless chicken breasts

6 chicken livers, deveined and chopped (optional)

150ml/5fl oz lime juice (about 6 big limes), plus 2 more limes, thinly sliced

handful of fresh coriander leaves, roughly chopped

1 avocado, stoned, peeled and sliced

A hearty salad from the Landes region of south-west France. There are a million quacking variations on the same theme, with some cooks adding foie gras, gizzards and confit duck. Paula Wolfert, in The Cooking of South West France, *says the original recipe called for 'the two very small fillets behind each whole duck breast …'. But she points out that only restaurants with a vast turnover of duck breasts could gather enough of these fillets for a salad. You want the meat hot, and the rest of the salad cool.*

Salade Landaise

SERVES 4

2 tbsp duck or goose fat (or olive oil)

½ garlic clove

1 thick slice of stale country bread, crusts removed, cut into cubes

2 duck breasts, skinned, trimmed of excess fat and cut lengthwise into strips

head of curly endive, refrigerated

bunch of watercress, thick stems removed, refrigerated

6 tomatoes, quartered

DRESSING

1 banana shallot, finely chopped

1 tbsp finely chopped fresh parsley

1 tbsp finely chopped fresh chives

1 tbsp finely chopped fresh chervil (optional)

1 tbsp lemon juice

sea salt and freshly ground black pepper

4 tbsp extra virgin olive oil

Heat 1 tbsp duck fat, add the garlic and bread, and cook over a medium–high heat for 3–4 minutes, until crisp and golden. Drain the croûtons on kitchen paper, discarding the garlic, and set aside.

To make the dressing, mix the shallot and herbs with the lemon juice and a good pinch of salt and pepper, then beat in the olive oil.

Heat the remaining 1 tbsp duck fat in a frying pan, season the duck well, and sauté over a high heat for 2–3 minutes, until well browned but still pink inside. Lightly toss the duck with the endive, watercress, tomatoes and croûtons. Divide among four bowls, then dress and serve immediately.

This is one of my favourite London restaurant dishes, which I've adapted from the classic served at E&O in Notting Hill. On paper, it sounds a little odd, self-conscious even. But those great dumb pink watery cubes not only add texture and tropical cool, but soak up the flavours too. Crisp duck, cool watermelon. Nice.

Crisp Duck and Watermelon Salad

Place a frying pan over a medium heat and cook the duck breasts, skin-side down, for 3–4 minutes, until the skin is golden and crisp. Transfer to a board and leave to cool.

To make the dressing, mix all the ingredients together in a small bowl and set aside.

Cut the duck breasts into 2.5cm/1-inch cubes. Heat 4–5cm/1½–2 inches of oil in a deep pan to about 170°C/340°F, or until a cube of bread turns golden in 30 seconds; alternatively, use an electric deep-fryer. Deep-fry the duck in three batches, until crisp, about 2–3 minutes. Drain briefly on kitchen paper.

Mix together the watermelon, radishes, bean sprouts, watercress, herbs, spring onions and cashews. Add the duck and dressing, toss lightly, and serve.

SERVES 4

3 duck breasts, skin on

groundnut or sunflower oil for deep-frying

450g/1lb watermelon, peeled, deseeded and cut into 3cm/1¼-inch cubes

100g/3½oz red radishes, thinly sliced

40g/1½oz bean sprouts, rinsed

2 handfuls of watercress, thick stems removed

large handful of fresh mint leaves

large handful of fresh coriander leaves

4 spring onions, sliced diagonally

50g/1¾oz unsalted cashews, dry-roasted

DRESSING

1 tbsp fish sauce

2 tbsp lime juice

1 tbsp dark soy sauce

2 bird's-eye chillies, finely chopped

½ tsp palm sugar (or caster sugar)

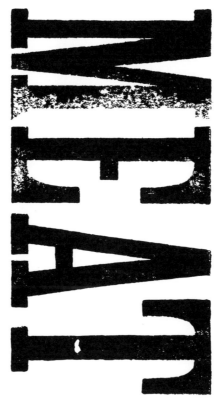

MEAT
as Seasoning

Meat as Seasoning. Not pepper, or salt, or a pinch of what-you-will. But beef stock and cured pig, a few charred nuggets of chorizo, or eggs baked with the remains of Sunday lunch's gravy. This is a chapter all about subtle additions, and savoury succour, using ingredients that won't break any bank.

It's hardly a revolutionary concept. The vast majority of the world's population cooks in a similar fashion. Outside the West, meat is still an expensive luxury, and meat as seasoning is not so much a choice as a way of life. And for hundreds of years in Britain, the prime cuts were reserved for the rich and royal, while the poor subsisted on pottage, a thick, rather dreary soup flavoured with the odd piece of cured pig.

Every culture has dishes in which scraps of beef, lamb, pork or chicken are eked out, giving depth and succour to staple dishes such as beans and rice. In Thailand, the vast and wonderful range of *priks* or relishes are there to add life and flavour to rice and raw vegetables, and often have small bits of pork pounded in.

The art of much Far Eastern and Deep Southern cooking is about extracting every last molecule of flavour from the cheapest and most unassuming of ingredients. Green beans with a little pork mince (*see* page 123), black-eyed peas with salt pork (*see* page 125). Of course, these dishes stand on their own two feet without the meat, a wonderful mouthful rather than some parsimonious bite. But by using meat to season instead of playing the starring role, you can raid the butcher's with minimum distress to your credit card.

The recipes might be thrifty, but they're never mean. Minced beef in Joe's Special (*see* page 121) and pupusas from El Salvador (*see* page 126). Rice, pasta, noodles and stocks. 'Gray pays' (*see* page 143) is a particular favourite, a Black Country classic that takes its flavour from bacon and a stock cube.

There's nothing overly fiddly or complex, and many of these dishes can be put together in minutes. But to truly understand meat cookery, one must grasp the basics of flavour. Boiled beans can be very dull indeed. But throw in a piece of cured pork, and things begin to taste rather more rosy. I want to prove that meat as seasoning can be every bit as delectable as meat on its tod. Hundreds of millions of people manage to turn the most lowly ingredients into something altogether more exciting. Meat needn't be the headline-grabbing star. Here, its influence is subtle but nevertheless profound.

This demure and economical mash-up is a Scottish classic, originally mixing just potatoes, onions and dripping. Lady Clark of Tillypronie's recipe, from the start of the twentieth century, advises thick-sliced, 'mealy' potatoes. Later versions include leftover meat too. But when judging the British Street Food Awards in 2013, I tasted a version made with slow-cooked shin, and finished with a blob of dill-spiked sour cream. Made by a pair of fine cooks called Katie Houston and Kim Clegg of Katie and Kim's Kitchen in Bristol, we decided it was the best dish of them all. This is my take on their version. Dripping is traditional, and essential if you don't include the meat. But butter is a decent alternative.

Stovies

SERVES 4

50g/1¾oz dripping or butter

2 onions, chopped

200g/7oz beef shin or braising steak, trimmed of excess fat and cut into 2.5cm/1-inch chunks

850g/1lb 14oz floury potatoes, peeled and sliced as thick as a £1 coin

150ml/5fl oz beef or chicken stock (cube is fine)

sea salt and freshly ground black pepper

100ml/3½fl oz sour cream, to serve

small pinch of chopped fresh dill, to serve

4 oatcakes, thickly buttered, to serve

Melt the dripping in a heavy casserole, add the onions and cook for 10 minutes, until soft.

Add the beef, potatoes and stock, plus salt and pepper, and cook, with the lid on, for 2½–3 hours, until the meat is falling apart.

Serve hot, with a blob of sour cream mixed with dill, and buttered oatcakes.

This is a San Francisco classic, born in the 1920s at New Joe's, an Italian-American red sauce sort of place. Late one night, the legend goes, a hungry jazzer walked in and ordered a spinach omelette. But he wanted a little something extra, to make it a proper dinner. You know, some meat or something. 'Gimme more', he drawled (allow me a little artistic licence; this account, like The Texas Chainsaw Massacre, *is 'based on a true story'). So the short-order chef chucked in hamburger meat and garlic. And Joe's Special was born. Or so they say. Anyway, it's a dish that fits pretty much any time of the day. Every Joe's in San Francisco still has it on the menu. Most pretend it's theirs, and their's alone.*

Joe's Special

Heat the oil in a large frying pan over a medium heat, add the onion and garlic and cook for 10 minutes, until soft.

Turn up the heat, add the minced beef and cook until browned, about 5 minutes. Add the spinach and cook for 2–3 minutes, stirring often, until totally wilted. If necessary, drain off any excess liquid.

Season the eggs well, pour over the spinach and cook for 3–4 minutes, until just cooked but still creamy.

Take off the heat and sprinkle with the Parmesan. Serve with crusty bread and a glass of punchy red wine.

SERVES 4

2 tbsp olive oil
1 onion, finely chopped
3 garlic cloves, finely chopped
200g/7oz minced beef
300g/10½oz spinach, trimmed
    and shredded
8 large eggs, lightly beaten
sea salt and freshly ground
    black pepper
25g/1oz Parmesan, finely
    grated
crusty bread, to serve

I love this dish, just green beans with minced pork, chillies and Sichuan pepper. It can be a side, but it also makes a decent dinner.

Sichuan Green Beans

Heat the oil in a wok or frying pan until smoking, add the beans and cook for 6–10 minutes, until they become soft and wrinkled, with brown spots. Remove with a slotted spoon and drain on kitchen paper.

Add the peppercorns and fry for 10 seconds. Add the garlic, chillies and spring onions and fry for another 10 seconds. Add the minced pork and fry for 1 minute, using two wooden spoons to break up the meat.

Return the beans to the pan along with the soy sauce and cook for another 30 seconds, or until the mince is cooked. Serve hot.

SERVES 4

2 tbsp groundnut or
    sunflower oil
500g/1lb 2oz green beans,
    trimmed
½ tbsp Sichuan peppercorns,
    roughly crushed
2 garlic cloves, finely chopped
5–10 dried red chillies
1 fresh red chilli
4 spring onions, chopped,
    white part only
150g/5½oz minced pork
big splash of soy sauce

Quite a mouthful, in every way, and proof that not all German food is cured pig and fermented cabbage. The Germans are porcine maestros. This is winter grub, rich and creamy, and studded with, yup, you've guessed it, cured pig. But not too much.

Schinkennudeln (Ham Noodles)

SERVES 4

300ml/10fl oz sour cream

2 large egg yolks

100g/3½oz Gruyère, finely grated

150g/5½oz good smoked ham, chopped or torn into pieces

300g/10½oz dried tagliatelle or flat, thickish noodles

sea salt

6 tbsp fresh white breadcrumbs

25g/1oz butter

Preheat your grill to medium–high. Put the sour cream in a bowl, then whisk in the egg yolks and stir in the Gruyère and ham.

Cook the tagliatelle in salted boiling water until al dente, then drain and return to the pan. Add the cream and ham sauce and toss.

Warm a wide flameproof dish, large enough to hold the pasta, and tip in the pasta and sauce. Sprinkle with breadcrumbs and dot with butter, then grill for 5 minutes.

No, not that popular beat combo with the fella with the txt spk name, but a Southern classic, and a staple of soul food. In the Deep South, white folk feasted on the prime cuts, while poor black slaves got by on scraps from the masters' table. This dish uses minimal meat. If you can get hold of salt pork, then great. Otherwise, use ham hock or a hunk of cured ham. Black-eyed peas, or cowpeas, came to the US with the slaves from Africa. I've added onion and bay leaf — not strictly authentic.

Black-Eyed Peas

Drain the peas, place in a large, heavy casserole, and cover with 1.5 litres/2½ pints cold water. Add the onion, bay leaf, chilli and salt pork. Bring to the boil, boil for 5 minutes, then simmer for 1–1½ hours, or until the beans are tender but not falling apart. Season with salt and pepper to taste.

SERVES 4

250g/9oz dried black-eyed
   peas, soaked in cold water
   overnight
1 onion, quartered
1 bay leaf
1 long dried red chilli
125g/4½oz salt pork, ham
   hock or cooked ham
sea salt and freshly ground
   black pepper

These fat, stuffed tortillas are probably the national dish of El Salvador, although it's hardly a culinary destination. But a great friend is half-Salvadorean and grew up there. She says they're sold on every street corner, from pupuserías *both fixed and mobile. And served with* curtido, *a sort of Latin American coleslaw that cuts a dashing swathe though all that lovely stodge. As for filling, you can stuff in what you want, cheese, meat or vegetables. This recipe is just a guide.*

Pupusas

SERVES 4

50g/1¾oz cooking chorizo, skinned, or smoked streaky bacon
about 2 tbsp groundnut or sunflower oil
100g/3½oz Cheddar or Gruyère, finely grated
1 small red or green chilli, finely chopped (optional)
250g/9oz masa harina (maize flour) (available from www.coolchile.co.uk)
400ml/14fl oz warm water
sea salt

CURTIDO

½ small cabbage, shredded
1 carrot, grated
1 small red onion, thinly sliced
125ml/4fl oz cider vinegar
pinch of caster sugar
1 jalapeño chilli, finely chopped (optional)

To make the *curtido*, put the cabbage, carrot and onion in a bowl. Pour over just-boiled water to cover and leave for 2 minutes. Drain and press out and discard the liquid. Put the vegetables back in the bowl and mix with the vinegar, sugar, a big pinch of salt, and the chilli, if using. Leave for at least 2 hours or, ideally, overnight.

Fry the chorizo in a frying pan over a medium–high heat for 3–4 minutes, using two wooden spoons to break up the meat very thoroughly. (Alternatively, fry the bacon until crisp, adding a little oil if necessary, then crumble finely.) Transfer to a plate and leave to cool before mixing with the grated cheese and chilli, if using.

Mix the masa with the water and a pinch of salt to make a soft, not too dry, dough. It should have the consistency of putty. Cover and leave to rest for 10 minutes.

Divide the dough into four portions and roll each into a ball. Make a hole, using your thumb, deep enough to take a spoonful of meat filling. Add the filling, pinch the dough over to seal, then flatten to a disc in your hands. Roll out using a rolling pin until 8–10mm/½ inch thick (putting it between two sheets of baking parchment makes it easier to roll).

Heat ½ tbsp oil in a frying pan over a highish heat and cook the *pupusas*, one at a time, for 3 minutes on each side, until crisp and golden. Keep warm in a low oven while you cook the rest, adding ½ tbsp oil each time. Serve with *curtido*.

Sicily is one hell of a place to eat in the spring. The citrus trees are in full bloom, the markets are verdant with baby artichokes, broad beans and peas, and the air has a sort of priapic tang that stirs the senses and fills the soul with joy. There are few lunches to beat those broad beans and peas, eaten with a great hunk of fresh pecorino and washed down with a cooling draught of icy local white. Bliss. My friend Luca, who grew up in Lipari, always used to cook it, too. You can go for some serious smoked pancetta, along with fresh peas. But the joy is that you can also use frozen peas and pancetta from the supermarket. The former might have a little more oomph and depth, but the latter is pretty decent. A grating of lemon zest adds zing.

Spaghetti with Peas, Pancetta and Mint

SERVES 4

sea salt and freshly ground
   black pepper
400g/14oz spaghetti
1 tbsp olive oil
1 garlic clove, peeled and
   lightly bashed with the flat
   of a knife
125g/4½oz smoked pancetta,
   cut into matchstick strips (or
   use lardons)
200g/7oz fresh or frozen peas
finely grated zest of
   1 unwaxed lemon
handful of fresh mint, roughly
   chopped
75g/2¾ oz pecorino or
   Parmesan, finely grated

Bring a large pan of water to the boil, add plenty of salt, then cook the pasta until al dente.

Meanwhile, heat the oil in a pan over a medium heat and cook the garlic for a few minutes, until lightly coloured, then remove. Do not let it burn.

Add the pancetta and fry until crisp. Then throw in the peas and cook for 1 minute. Turn off the heat and add the lemon zest and mint.

Drain the pasta and mix with the sauce, season with lots of pepper and sprinkle with pecorino. Serve at once.

Bugger Paris in the spring; Rome's where it's at. Artichokes, peas, puntarelle and broad beans flood the market stalls. And this dish, traditionally made with guanciale, *cured pig's cheek, is everywhere. If you can be shagged, shell the beans (the skin can sometimes be bitter). But the pork is hardly shy and retiring when it comes to flavour, so it's not really necessary. If* guanciale *is impossible to get, substitute pancetta.*

Broad Beans with Guanciale

Heat the oil in a pan over a medium–high heat and fry the pork and onion until the pork begins to crisp and the onion is golden, about 12 minutes.

Add the beans and cook for 1 minute. Turn up the heat, throw in the wine and leave to bubble for 5 minutes. Season and serve at once.

SERVES 4

1 tbsp olive oil
250g/9oz *guanciale* or
    pancetta, cut into cubes
1 small onion, finely chopped
2kg/4lb 8oz fresh broad beans,
    podded, or 550g/1lb 4oz
    frozen baby broad beans
250ml/9fl oz dry white wine
sea salt and freshly ground
    black pepper

This is my take on Acelgas con papa y chorizo, *a Mexican side dish that mixes chard with potatoes and chorizo. Spinach is easier to find than chard, but does have a rather different taste and texture. In season, round about late summer, I tend to substitute chard for the spinach. Just remove the stems, wash, place in a saucepan with the water that clings to the leaves, cover and cook for 4 minutes, then chop and treat like spinach.*

Spinach with Potatoes and Chorizo

SERVES 4–6 AS A SIDE DISH

450g/1lb floury potatoes,
   peeled and cut into
   2cm/¾-inch chunks
salt
2 tbsp olive oil
300g/10½oz cooking chorizo,
   sliced as thick as a £1 coin
1 onion, chopped
700g/1lb 9oz tomatoes,
   roughly chopped
1kg/2lb 4oz spinach, trimmed
   and shredded

Parboil the potatoes in lightly salted water for 5 minutes, then drain.

Heat 1 tbsp oil in a deep pan and cook the chorizo until crisp. Remove with a slotted spoon, then add the onion and cook in the chorizo fat until soft. Add another 1 tbsp oil, then add the potatoes and cook over a medium heat until some burnished edges appear.

Add the tomatoes and a pinch of salt, then reduce the heat slightly and cook for 10 minutes.

Add the spinach and cook for 2 minutes, stirring regularly. Serve hot.

Rice and peas with a Venetian accent. It's also the main offering to St Mark the Evangelist, the city's patron saint and served up on 25 April. The recipe varies little, using fresh peas, good stock, risotto rice, pancetta and Parmesan. I love the introduction to the recipe in Russell Norman's Polpo, *the best book on Venetian eating in the English language. 'This is not one of those dishes where frozen peas will do', he warns. 'Absolutely not. Sorry. You must use fresh peas. And you must shell them.' You need fresh stock too. I love a shortcut as much as the next indolent cook. But certain dishes just must be done right.*

Risi e Bisi

SERVES 6

1.5kg/3lb 5oz peas in pods
1.5 litres/2½ pints fresh light
   chicken stock (*see* page 223)
50g/1¾oz butter
1 onion, finely chopped
125g/4½oz pancetta, cut into
   small cubes
500g/1lb 2oz carnaroli rice
big handful of grated
   Parmesan
small handful of fresh parsley,
   roughly chopped
sea salt and freshly ground
   black pepper

Pod the peas and set aside. Chop up the pods and simmer for 20 minutes in the stock. Strain and discard the pulpy pods.

Melt the butter in a large, heavy casserole, then add the onion and cook over a low heat until soft. Add the pancetta and cook gently for 5 or so minutes.

Add the peas and cook for 2 minutes. Add the pea-pod broth, bring back to the boil and simmer for 5 minutes.

Throw in the rice, cover and simmer gently for 20 minutes. It should be sloppy, but still with the merest core of bite within each grain.

Add the Parmesan and parsley, stir, cover and leave for 5 minutes to relax. Season and serve. Eat with a spoon.

A good Sunday lunch should sprawl into early evening, meaning that dinner should be suitably light. I came up with this when all we had left was a little gravy and some eggs. Spare gravy is a rare thing, so I suggest putting a little aside before it goes on the table.

Sunday Night Gravy-Baked Eggs

Preheat the oven to fan 180°C/350°F/Gas 6. Break the eggs into four ramekins, dribble in 2 tsp of gravy and 2 tsp cream and put a piece of butter in each. Season well.

Put the ramekins into a small roasting pan and add just-boiled water to come halfway up them. Bake for 8–10 minutes, until the white is just set and the yolk still liquid.

Serve with white bread, toasted and cut into soldiers.

SERVES 4

4 eggs
3 tbsp leftover thick gravy (if yours is thin, boil to reduce and thicken)
3 tbsp single cream
20g/¾oz butter, cut into 4 pieces
sea salt and freshly ground black pepper
white bread, to serve

Savoury jelly. I love the stuff; millions disagree. Wobbling, seductive and shimmering, it contains the very quintessence of meaty allure. Throw in an oozing egg, wrapped in a piece of good ham, and you have a truly magnificent mouthful. It's an increasingly rare sight on London's menus these days. Café Anglais used to do a perfect version, but now only Bellamy's in Mayfair provides my jellied fix. When in Paris, go to Chez Georges, just off Place des Victoires. It's the ultimate version. This recipe might look a little complex, but it's not difficult. Use a good dark chicken stock and there's no need for gelatine.

Oeufs en Gelée

SERVES 4

800ml reduced fresh dark chicken stock (*see* page 226), left to cool so it turns to jelly

1 egg white

6 sheets of gelatine (if not using a really good, reduced stock)

dash of dry sherry

4 sprigs of fresh tarragon

4 eggs

4 thin slices of good smoked ham

Heat the stock gently in a pan and whisk in the egg white. Turn up the heat to a gentle simmer and leave for 20 minutes. A dirty white crust will form, filled with all the impurities. Lift off the crust using a slotted spoon, then strain the stock through a muslin-lined sieve for gleaming purity.

If your stock was not jellified, you will need to use gelatine. Soak the gelatine in cold water for 5–10 minutes, then squeeze out excess water. Add the gelatine to the hot stock and stir until it dissolves completely.

Add the sherry to the stock and leave to cool.

Put a sprig of tarragon, torn into pieces, into each of four large ramekins or teacups, then pour 1cm/½ inch of stock into each one, cover and chill in the fridge for 30 minutes, or until beginning to set.

Poach the eggs so they are still soft, then carefully lift out of the water using a slotted spoon and drain on a clean tea towel. Leave until cold. (You can alternatively soft boil and then peel the eggs.)

When the eggs are cold, remove the ramekins from the fridge. Add a slice of ham and 1 egg per ramekin, and fill with the rest of the jellied stock. Leave in the fridge for a few hours to set.

When ready to serve, dip the ramekins into a bowl of boiling water for a few seconds, then turn out onto plates. Alternatively, serve in teacups without turning out.

A great Neapolitan dish and an example of the influence high French cooking had on grand Neapolitan kitchens in the eighteenth century. The name is a bastardised version of 'gateaux', and this is a rare southern Italian dish in which potatoes are the star, alongside massive amounts of butter and cheese. A little salami, too. It can be served as a side dish, but really it's a dish unto itself.

Gatto

SERVES 8

1kg/2lb 4oz floury potatoes, peeled and cut into chunks

50g/1¾oz butter, plus extra for greasing

60g/2¼oz dried breadcrumbs

150g/5½oz Parmesan, grated

150g/5½oz pecorino, grated

150g/5½oz soppressata, or other Neapolitan salami, cubed

1 large egg, beaten

handful of fresh parsley, finely chopped

salt

100ml/3½fl oz full-fat milk

2 x 125g/4½oz mozzarella balls, drained and torn into pieces

100g/3½oz smoked mozzarella, finely cubed (if you can find it – otherwise, use the same quantity of regular mozzarella)

Boil the potatoes in salted water until just soft, then drain and leave in the colander for 10 minutes.

Preheat the oven to fan 200°C/400°F/Gas 9. Butter a 23cm/9-inch springform cake tin and coat with half the breadcrumbs, tipping out any excess.

Pass the potatoes through a ricer or mouli (you can't just mash here) into a large bowl and mix with the Parmesan, pecorino, soppressata, egg, parsley and salt. Heat the milk over a low heat, add a quarter of the butter and, when it melts, pour into the potato mixture and stir firmly, but not too brutally.

Ladle two-thirds of the mixture into the prepared tin and gently smooth with a spatula or the back of a spoon.

Sprinkle with the mozzarella, keeping it away from the edge. Top with the remaining potato mixture and use a fork to mark a pattern on top. Sprinkle with the remaining breadcrumbs and dot with little shards of the remaining butter.

Bake for 30 minutes, until golden. Leave to stand for 15 minutes, then run a knife around the inside of the tin, turn out onto a board and hew into fat slices.

Don't worry. I'm not on some quixotic mission to drag you away from the Heinz version. They're perfect, needing just the merest dribble of Tabasco and Worcestershire sauce, as well as a flurry of fresh pepper, to be eaten cold, direct from the tin. Early colonists learned how to bake beans from the Native Americans, using a clay pot sunk into a pit lined with hot stones. They used bear fat for flavour, which could be a little tricky to get hold of these days. Pork will do just fine, either salt pork or unsmoked streaky bacon. Or a ham hock. Molasses or treacle adds rich, dark sweetness, while a little ginger, a recent embellishment, adds zing.

Real Baked Beans

SERVES 6

250g/9oz dried white haricot beans, soaked in cold water overnight, or 2 x 400g/14oz cans, rinsed and drained

1 onion, peeled and studded with 8 cloves (if using dried beans)

2 bay leaves (if using dried beans)

50g/1¾oz butter

300g/10½oz salt pork or unsmoked streaky bacon, chopped

1 large onion, chopped

3 garlic cloves, chopped

4 tbsp molasses or black treacle

100ml/3½fl oz tomato ketchup

2 tbsp tomato purée

40g/1½oz muscovado sugar

2 tsp mustard powder

2.5cm/1 inch piece of fresh ginger, peeled and grated

2–3 tsp Tabasco

big pinch of salt

If you are using soaked dried beans, drain and rinse them, then put in a large pan with 2 litres/3½ pints cold water along with the clove-studded onion and bay leaves. Bring to the boil for 5 minutes, then simmer until tender, about 1½ hours. Drain the beans, discarding the onion and bay leaves.

Preheat the oven to fan 160°C/325°F/Gas 4.

Heat the butter in a large heavy casserole and cook the bacon and onion for 10 minutes, until golden. Add the garlic and cook gently for a further minute.

Stir in the molasses, tomato ketchup, tomato purée, sugar, mustard, ginger and Tabasco. Simmer for about a minute.

Pour in the cooked or canned beans and 600ml/20fl oz cold water, mix gently, bring to a simmer, then cover and bake for about 1 hour. Remove the lid and bake for another 30 minutes. The beans should be thick and wet. Serve hot.

No, not under-aged potatoes, but a dish from a small Parisian bistro called Juveniles, owned by a charming Scottish fella. My memory (entirely happy) of the place is pretty hazy, but I do remember haggis being on the menu. Along with a mighty dish made with spuds, raclette cheese and bacon. It was, as you'd expect, as good as Alpine cheese mixed with spuds and bacon can be.

Potatoes Juveniles

Put the potatoes in a pan, cover with cold water, salt generously and bring to the boil over a high heat. Reduce the heat to medium and cook until the potatoes are just soft, 10–15 minutes. Drain and cool, then cut into 8mm/⅜-inch slices.

Cook the bacon in a heavy-bottomed pan over a medium heat until crisp, adding a glug of olive oil if necessary. Drain on kitchen paper and set aside.

Preheat the grill to high and divide the potatoes between four ovenproof plates, so they overlap slightly. Season with black pepper and a little cayenne, then sprinkle with the bacon and cover with the cheese. Put the plates under the grill until the cheese melts, bubbles and browns, 8–10 minutes. Sprinkle with parsley before serving.

SERVES 4

500g/1lb 2oz waxy new
    potatoes
sea salt and freshly ground
    black pepper
125g/4½oz smoked lardons, or
    streaky bacon, cut into small
    pieces
big pinch of cayenne pepper
225g/8oz raclette cheese,
    thinly sliced
1 tbsp finely chopped flat-leaf
    parsley

No-nonsense-noshing, and made better still by a few nuggets of crisp bacon or pancetta. The key is to go big on the sauce. There's little more disappointing than a golden, bubbling macaroni cheese that tastes of little more than buttery, uncooked flour. And remember to grease the dish well with butter.

Mac Cheese

SERVES 6

200g/7oz smoked streaky bacon, or pancetta, cut into 1.5cm/⅝-inch pieces

40g/1½oz butter, plus extra for greasing

40g/1½oz plain flour

600ml/20fl oz full-fat milk

175g/6oz good Cheddar, grated

175g/6oz Gruyère, Beaufort or Comté cheese, grated

salt and freshly ground black pepper

few drops of Tabasco

dribble of Worcestershire sauce

250g/9oz macaroni

50g/1¾oz Parmesan, finely grated

25g/1oz fresh white breadcrumbs

Preheat the oven to fan 180°C/350°F/Gas 6. Fry the bacon in a heavy-bottomed pan over a medium heat until crisp, adding a little olive oil if necessary. Drain on kitchen paper and set aside.

Melt the butter in a saucepan over a low heat, stir in the flour and cook gently for 3–4 minutes. Add the milk and whisk until there are no lumps; simmer for 5–10 minutes, until smooth and thick. Add the Cheddar and Gruyère and stir until melted, then add the pepper, Tabasco and Worcestershire sauce.

Cook the macaroni in salted boiling water until al dente; drain in a colander.

Tip the macaroni into a well-buttered baking dish, add the bacon, then pour over the sauce and mix. Mix the Parmesan with the breadcrumbs and scatter on top. Bake for 35–40 minutes, until bubbling, then serve.

At Harry's Bar in Venice, the tables might be tiny, but there are a few things they do here better than anywhere else in the world. The martini, for one, bone dry and served in a tiny glass of about three sips. Just as it should be. Otherwise it turns into warm spirits. And this dish, Tagliolini gratinati al prosciutto, *to give it its full title, the bastard child of Italy and France. What a beautiful bastard it is.*

Harry's Bar Pasta Gratin

SERVES 4

350g/12oz dried tagliolini or tagliatelle
50g/1¾oz butter
75g/2¾oz prosciutto, cut into thin strips
85g/3oz Parmesan, grated

BÉCHAMEL SAUCE
375ml/13fl oz full-fat milk
½ onion, peeled
1 bay leaf
25g/1oz butter
25g/1oz plain flour
salt and freshly ground black pepper

To make the béchamel, put the milk, onion and bay leaf in a pan and heat until it's just about to boil, then remove the onion and bay leaf using a slotted spoon and set the milk aside. Melt the butter in a saucepan and stir in the flour over a medium heat, until you have a smooth, just golden roux. Gradually add the hot milk, stirring all the time (I use a mini-whisk with a horseshoe-shaped twist of wire at the end) until the sauce is thick and velvety smooth. When it comes to the boil, stop stirring and cook gently for about 10 minutes. Add salt and pepper to taste. Set aside.

Bring a large pan of salted water to the boil, add the pasta and cook until al dente. Drain well.

Meanwhile, melt one-third of the butter in a pan over a medium heat, until foaming. Add the prosciutto and cook for 1 minute.

Add the pasta and another one-third of the butter, sprinkle with half the Parmesan and mix well.

Preheat the grill to hot. Put the pasta into a warmed 2-litre/3½-pint flameproof dish, spoon over the béchamel sauce and scatter the remaining Parmesan on top. Dot the remaining butter over the cheese.

Grill for 3–4 minutes, until golden and bubbling. Serve hot.

This recipe is based on one by my friend and business partner Graham Jebb, a great man in every way. He has one of the thickest Black Country accents you've ever heard, so 'grey peas' become 'gray pays'. This is classic Black Country cooking, economical but never mean.

Gray Pays

Preheat the oven to fan 150°C/300°F/Gas 3.

Fry the bacon in a large, heavy casserole over a medium heat until crisp, adding a glug of olive oil if necessary. Then add the onion and fry until soft, about 10 minutes.

Add the peas and barley and cover with 1 litre/1¾ pints cold water, crumble in the stock cube and add salt and pepper. Bring to the boil, then cover and cook in the oven for about 1½ hours, or until tender.

Remove from the oven and stir in the butter until well combined. Serve spread on crusty bread.

SERVES 4

10 rashers of good thick
   smoked streaky bacon (but
   the more the better, says
   Graham), cut into 2cm/
   ¾ inch pieces
1 large onion, sliced
225g/8oz dried grey peas
   (traditionally maple peas but
   you can use green or yellow
   dried peas too), rinsed
225g/8oz pearl barley, rinsed
1 beef stock cube
sea salt and freshly ground
   black pepper
25g/1oz butter
crusty bread, to serve

Salad dressing made with bacon drippings. Served hot, so it wilts the pristine green leaves onto which it's poured. In the Southern States they call this 'killed salad'. Not 'wilted', but 'killed'. Brilliant.

Killed Salad

SERVES 4

8 good thick fatty rashers of
   smoked streaky bacon
2–3 romaine lettuce hearts,
   pulled apart
3 tomatoes, each cut into
   6 wedges
½ red onion, thinly sliced

BACON VINAIGRETTE
2 tbsp white wine vinegar
1 tbsp runny honey
big pinch of mustard powder
sea salt and freshly ground
   black pepper
about 6 tbsp extra virgin olive
   oil

Fry the bacon in a heavy-bottomed pan over a medium heat until crisp, then drain on kitchen paper, pour off the fat and reserve for the dressing. Crumble the bacon.

To make the vinaigrette, heat the vinegar, honey, mustard, salt and pepper in a small pan until warm, then whisk in the reserved bacon fat and enough olive oil to make up to 100ml/3½fl oz, until smooth and emulsified.

Arrange the lettuce leaves in a bowl, add the tomatoes and red onion, sprinkle with the bacon, then pour over the hot dressing. The leaves should wilt. Eat sharpish.

Cornbread is a staple of the Southern States and, when done well, should be as yellow as a Kansas cornfield on harvest day, and light and airy too. Jalapeños add a little heat, and crumbled pork scratchings add, well, crunch and punch. I recommend Mr Trotter's Great British Pork Crackling. But as part-owner, I would, wouldn't I?

Jalapeño Cornbread

Preheat the oven to fan 180°C/350°F/Gas 6. Oil a 20 x 28cm/ 8 x 11-inch baking tin and heat for a couple of minutes in the oven.

Mix the cornmeal, salt and baking powder in a bowl.

In another bowl, mix together the remaining ingredients (except the scratchings). Add to the dry ingredients, stir well, and pour into the warmed tin. Bake for about 30 minutes, then scatter the pork scratchings over the top and bake for a further 10–20 minutes, until golden and springy to the touch. Leave to cool in the tin for 10 minutes, then cut into squares and serve.

MAKES 20 PIECES

250g/9oz fine yellow cornmeal

½ tsp fine salt

1 tsp baking powder

2 large eggs, beaten

250ml/9fl oz full-fat milk

85g/3oz pickled sliced jalapeños, drained

2 onions, finely chopped

125ml/4fl oz vegetable oil, plus extra for greasing

200g/7oz Cheddar, coarsely grated

60g/2¼oz bag of pork scratchings, crushed into small pieces

This is adapted from the great Richard Olney's recipe in Simple French Food, *which is simply superb. There's a touch of bitterness from the leaves, but a whole lot of richness too.*

Gratin of Chicory and Bacon

SERVES 6

50g/1¾oz butter

6 heads of chicory (white, red or a combination), discoloured outer leaves removed

sea salt and freshly ground black pepper

50g/1¾oz Parmesan, finely grated

100g/3½oz coarse fresh white breadcrumbs

3 tbsp chopped fresh parsley

100g/3½oz lean unsmoked bacon rashers, cut into 1cm/½-inch pieces

300ml/10fl oz double cream

lemon quarters, to serve

Preheat the oven to fan 210°C/415°F/Gas 8. Generously butter a large gratin dish.

Split the chicory in two lengthwise. Pack it into the gratin dish in a tight single layer, split side down, and sprinkle with salt and pepper.

Mix together the Parmesan, breadcrumbs, parsley and bacon, and scatter evenly over the surface.

Place the dish in the oven and, after a few minutes, turn the temperature down to fan 170°C/340°F/Gas 5. Bake for 30 minutes, then remove from the oven and trickle the cream around the sides of the gratin. Bake for another 30 minutes or so, trickling in more cream if it didn't all fit in first time, until bubbling and golden. Serve with lemon quarters.

It's rare I'll eschew a cob of freshly roasted corn, slathered with butter and pepper. Add a little hint of bacon, and this creamed version is pig-scented brilliance.

Creamed Corn and Bacon

SERVES 4

6 very fresh corn cobs, leaves
  removed
1 tbsp sunflower oil
5 rashers of smoked streaky
  bacon
25g/1oz butter
4 tbsp milk
sea salt and freshly ground
  black pepper

Hold the corn cobs vertically, then slice downwards with a sharp knife to cut off the kernels.

Heat the oil in a wide, heavy-bottomed pan over a medium heat. Fry the bacon for around 5 minutes, until crisp. Transfer the bacon to a plate and leave to cool, then crumble and set aside.

In the same pan, heat the bacon fat until hot and add the corn. Reduce the heat and add the butter and milk. Cook for about 10 minutes, until the corn is tender.

Increase the heat, and slightly brown the stuff on the bottom of the pan, but don't burn. Season to taste and serve topped with the bacon.

Whenever I'm in Mexico, these always turn up at breakfast in a silver-plated chafing dish. The tortillas are soft but not soggy, and served with a salsa fierce enough to blow last night's excess (or even restraint) away. It's a way of using up stale tortillas, as well as any leftover sauce and cheese. Of course, the use of leftover tortillas is not something that vexes the British cook. But this dish is well worth the effort. Proper tortillas are essential. There's no place for Doritos here.

Chilaquiles Rojos

Preheat the grill to red-hot. Put the tomatoes on the grill rack, add a dribble of oil and a little salt, and grill for 6–8 minutes, until the skins are blackened. Peel and set aside.

Put the chicken in a heavy-bottomed casserole and add about 1 litre/1¾ pints water, to cover. Add 2 garlic cloves, a big pinch of salt, half the onion and all the parsley. Bring to a simmer, then cover and cook for 10–12 minutes, or until the chicken is cooked through and there is no trace of pink in the juices when it is pierced with a skewer through the thickest part. Remove the chicken, leave to cool, then shred. Reserve 250ml/9fl oz of the broth.

Roughly chop the remaining onion half. Put the chillies and remaining 2 garlic cloves in a small pan of boiling water and simmer for 5 minutes. Drain, then put the boiled chillies (stalks removed) and garlic, the onion and roasted tomatoes in a blender with a big pinch of salt and the reserved broth. Blitz until very finely chopped.

Heat a little oil in a frying pan over a low–medium heat. Add the sauce and cook for 5 minutes. Turn the heat down to low, cover the pan loosely with a lid and cook for 10 minutes, stirring occasionally, until fairly thick. Season.

Meanwhile, cut each tortilla into six. Pour 1cm/½ inch of oil into a wide pan and heat to 180°C/350°F, or until a cube of bread browns in 30 seconds. Add one-third of the tortillas and fry for 1½–2 minutes, until crisp and golden. Drain on kitchen paper and repeat until all are cooked. Don't let the oil overheat.

Add the chicken to the sauce and warm for 30 seconds, then add the tortillas. Top with the crème fraîche and cheese and cook for a few minutes without stirring. Scatter over the herbs.

SERVES 6

750g/1lb 10oz tomatoes
vegetable or groundnut oil
sea salt and freshly ground
    black pepper
1 skinless, boneless chicken
    breast
4 garlic cloves, peeled
1 onion, peeled and halved
6 sprigs of fresh parsley
6 serrano chillies (or, if you
    can't find them, jalapeños)
12–16 soft maize tortillas
250ml/9fl oz crème fraîche
60g/2¼oz queso fresco
    (available from www.
    coolchile.co.uk) or, failing
    that, feta, crumbled
handful of fresh coriander,
    roughly chopped

Chinese by birth, a native of Fujian province, this red-flecked beauty has made Singapore (where the province of Penang is) and Malaysia its home. It's classic hawker food, a rich, chilli-spiked scarlet broth, stuffed with egg noodles, fat prawns, slivers of chicken, hard-boiled egg and even pork knuckles and ribs. The key is the broth, flavoured with pork bones and fried prawn heads (freeze the heads and shells of any prawns you eat until you have a decent-sized bag). Oh, and the all-important sambal, slightly stinky, rather hot but utterly essential.

Penang Prawn Mee

SERVES 6

2 cooked chicken carcasses
600g/1lb 5oz pork bones
2kg/4lb 8oz raw prawns in
　shells
1 tbsp groundnut oil
3 garlic cloves, finely chopped
2 lemongrass stalks
2.5cm/1-inch piece of fresh
　ginger, peeled and sliced
100g/3½oz dried shrimps

SAMBAL BELACHAN

25 small dried red chillies,
　deseeded and soaked in just-
　boiled water for 20 minutes
10 shallots, roughly chopped
5 garlic cloves, chopped
15g/½oz belachan (shrimp
　paste)
6 tbsp groundnut oil

TO SERVE

2 tsp sea salt flakes
2 tsp caster sugar
225g/8oz dried egg noodles
150g/5½oz dried rice
　vermicelli, cooked
150g/5½oz kangkung or pak
　choi, blanched
150g/5½oz bean sprouts,
　blanched
6 hard-boiled eggs, quartered
4 skinless, boneless chicken
　breasts, very thinly sliced

Put the chicken carcasses and pork bones in a large pot, cover with 2 litres/3½ pints of water and bring to the boil. Skim off any scum, then turn the heat down to a simmer.

Remove the heads and shells from the prawns and set aside. Devein the prawns and set aside in the fridge.

Heat the oil in a wide pan over a low heat and cook the garlic for a few minutes. Add the prawn shells and heads and cook for 5 minutes, until the oil turns a deep orange and shells are slightly charred. Tip the contents of the pan into the stockpot, bring back to the boil, skim and then simmer for about 1 hour. Half the lemongrass stalks lengthwise, then add them, the ginger and dried shrimps to the pot and simmer for 1 hour.

To make the sambal, or chilli paste, blend all the ingredients together in a food processor, then cook in a wok or pan over a low heat for about 10 minutes. (Do this in a well-ventilated area or with the extractor on full.)

When the stock is ready, add half the paste (or more or less, to taste) and stir well. Add the salt and sugar and taste. Traditionally, the soup should be a little salty. Strain through muslin or a fine sieve into a clean pan and bring to a simmer.

Cook the noodles and vermicelli according to the packet instructions, then drain, rinse and leave to cool. Divide them between six deep serving bowls, then add a handful of blanched greens and bean sprouts and an egg to each.

Add the chicken to the stock and simmer for 1 minute. Add the prawns and simmer for 1–2 minutes, until pink and the chicken and prawns are cooked through. Immediately pour the hot stock into the bowls and serve with the remaining sambal belachan on the side.

Green and deeply pleasant, this dish is the very essence of spring's fecundity, a verdant riot of priapic youth. It's a strictly seasonal recipe, devoured in Italy at this time of year. In the UK it's more of an early summer feast, when the market stalls are sagging under the weight of peas, broad beans, asparagus and minuscule artichokes. A homemade stock is key, but a light one, so as not to bludgeon all this pert finery.

Risotto Primavera

Briefly blanch the peas, broad beans, asparagus and artichokes in salted boiling water, then drain. Cut the asparagus into short lengths. Set aside.

Bring the stock to a rolling boil in a pan.

Meanwhile, melt 25g/1oz of the butter in a heavy-bottomed pan, along with the olive oil. Add the onion and cook gently for 5 minutes, until softened.

Add the rice and cook for a couple of minutes, stirring, until the grains are well coated in butter and oil.

Add a ladle of boiling stock and stir until absorbed. Repeat every time the rice has drunk in the stock, stirring constantly but not obsessively. The rice will take anything from 15 to 25 minutes to cook: it should be plump and tender, still keeping its shape, with the merest core of bite in each grain.

Take off the heat and leave to rest for a minute. Then beat in the cold butter, followed by the Parmesan. Really give it hell, beating with a wooden spoon until it is one glorious flowing whole.

Add the vegetables and heat through for a couple of minutes, stirring occasionally. Stir in a little more hot stock if the mixture doesn't flow easily once everything is hot. Add the parsley, stir, and serve immediately, scattered with the Parmesan shavings.

SERVES 6

200g/7oz freshly podded peas

200g/7oz freshly podded baby broad beans

200g/7oz slender asparagus, tough stalks removed

200g/7oz fresh artichoke hearts, thinly sliced

1.2 litres/2 pints fresh light chicken stock (*see* page 223)

125g/4½oz butter, cold and cubed

2 tbsp olive oil

1 small onion, finely chopped

300g/10½oz arborio or carnaroli rice

100g/3½oz Parmesan, finely grated, plus extra, thinly shaved, to serve

handful of fresh parsley, finely chopped

Most agree that jerk was born in Jamaica. It was originally a pork dish, a leftover from the Spanish conquest of the Caribbean. Another less happy reminder of their rule were the Maroons, African slaves left behind by the Spanish and, in the eighteenth century, hunted mercilessly by the British. They needed to take their meat on the run, so concocted a seasoning from readily available ingredients. It not only preserved the meat, but flavoured it too – the sweet, clovey tang of allspice, and the fierce, fruity beauty of the Scotch bonnet chilli. All cooked over a fire of pimento wood. The jerk seasoning below, adapted from a recipe in Virginia Burke's Eat Caribbean, *will work with pork, chicken, sea bass and corn on the cob.*

Jerk Chicken Soup

SERVES 4

2 skinless, boneless chicken
   breasts
100ml/3½fl oz Jerk marinade
   (see below)
100g/3½oz long-grain rice
1.5 litres/2½ pints fresh light
   chicken stock (*see page 223*)
150g/5½oz baby spinach or
   85g/3oz spinach leaves,
   trimmed and shredded
juice of 1 lime
1 Scotch bonnet pepper, sliced
   into rounds

JERK MARINADE

5 spring onions, trimmed and
   roughly chopped
2–4 Scotch bonnet chillies,
   stalks removed
2 tsp allspice berries
½ cinnamon stick, bashed
1 tbsp chopped fresh thyme
1 tsp grated nutmeg
1 tsp brown sugar
1½ tsp sea salt
big grind of black pepper
big glug of groundnut oil
75ml/2½fl oz white wine
   vinegar

Cut the chicken into 1.5cm/⅝-inch slices, put in a non-reactive dish and pour over the marinade. Cover and marinate in the fridge for 2 hours.

Cook the rice according to the packet instructions, then drain.

Meanwhile, heat the stock until simmering. Lift the pieces of chicken out of the marinade, add to the stock and simmer for 3–5 minutes, until cooked through with no signs of pink in the juices of the thickest slice when it is cut in half. Add the spinach and lime juice and cook until the spinach wilts.

Put a handful of the cooked rice into each of four bowls, ladle in the soup and chicken, and garnish with a slice of Scotch bonnet, then serve.

Jerk marinade

Put all the ingredients except the vinegar into a large mortar and bash with a pestle to make a paste. Or throw into a food processor and blitz to a paste. Stir in the vinegar. Cover and store in the fridge for up to three days.

So simple. And such flavour. Although you must use a homemade stock, you can use frozen peas.

Chicken, Pea and Watercress Soup

Bring the stock to the boil in a large pan. Add the potato and simmer until nearly cooked, about 5–10 minutes. Crush the odd lump.

Add the meat, thyme and lemon juice, and season. Add the watercress and peas and bring back to the boil. Serve with crusty bread.

SERVES 4

850ml/1½ pints fresh light
   chicken stock (*see* page 223)
1 large floury potato, peeled
   and diced
meat from the cooked stock
   bones, skinned and shredded
leaves from 1 sprig of thyme
juice of ½ lemon
sea salt and freshly ground
   black pepper
250g/9oz watercress, trimmed
   and roughly chopped
250g/9oz peas
crusty bread, to serve

Silken yet substantial, this is broth with balls, a good chicken stock with 'little shreds' of egg and a healthy dose of Parmesan. It comes from Lazio, but you'll now find it all over Italy. The key to this dish is the broth, as rich and hearty as possible; I use a reduced dark chicken stock.

Stracciatella

Mix the Parmesan, eggs, parsley, nutmeg and pepper in a bowl with a splash of the stock.

Bring the rest of the stock to the boil in a pan, then reduce the heat to medium and stir with a whisk in a clockwise direction. Slowly add the egg and Parmesan mixture, stirring with the whisk a couple more times, then take off the heat. Leave the eggs to cook in the hot stock until just thickened and silky. Serve immediately.

SERVES 4

50g/1¾oz Parmesan, finely
    grated
4 large eggs, lightly beaten
large handful of flat-leaf
    parsley, roughly chopped
a small grating of nutmeg
freshly ground black pepper
1 litre/1¾ pints reduced
    fresh dark chicken stock
    (*see* page 226)

Wild MEAT & OFFAL

Variety meat. Organs. Guts. Offal. With names like this, it's little wonder that all these (mainly) wonderful bits and bobs inspire revulsion and hate. Too visceral, they say, too fierce and frightening and, well, you know, odd. As if munching on great slabs of muscle is utterly civilised, while the softer, sexier, altogether more interesting parts of the beast are abhorrent. Well, no matter. I'm not here to try and convince the naysayers and fusspots about the joys of quick-fried kidneys and slow-cooked tripe. Or gently poached calf's brains in a great puddle of spiky *beurre noisette*.

For me, and millions of others, offal is a true pleasure. Not poo-scented andouillettes (I don't care how much mustard they slather on, I still can't get beyond that scatological stink) or Laotian raw tripe salad (challenging, to say the least, like meaty chewing gum, with a slight honk of rotting flesh). And certainly not great tube-infested slabs of ox liver, cooked until school-issue dark grey and possessing all the appeal of puke soup.

No, I mean oxtail daube (*see* page 164) and crisp pig's ears (*see* page 170), chicken liver pâté (*see* page 171) and kidneys in sherry (*see* page 168). Because offal's fundamental problem is not one of taste or texture, rather simple perception. Most of us haven't grown up with the stuff, therefore it scares us. Chicken breast and fillet steak are fine and respectable. Spleen sandwiches and ducks' tongues many miles removed.

In the West, we tend towards the bland and predictable. But in countries where meat remains an expensive luxury (especially the prime cuts), not a piece of the beast is wasted. And these parts are relished. One sip of *menudo*, a classic hangover-blasting Mexican stew filled with tripe and chillies and trotters, is enough to rocket one into the nascent day. As are Sichuan fire-exploded kidneys and Korean slow-cooked beef tendon. These dishes are as much about texture as they are taste; cheap, nourishing and endlessly splendid.

Closer to home, kidneys are joyous, ever-giving lobes of sweet, slightly scented softness. I'm obsessed with that texture, with just the right amount of give. Sliced roasted heart tastes like exceptional steak, while sweetbreads (thymus and pancreas) are as rich as a podgy oligarch, and a thousand times more appealing. All have flavours and textures that you'd never dream of finding in the more everyday (and expensive) cuts.

Give offal a chance. Start with chicken liver pâté, spread thick across toast, before moving on to a more personal encounter with kidneys, cooked gently in sherry (*see* page 168). Or drowned in a thick béchamel sauce (*see* page 169). Before you know it, you'll be romping among brains and digging beautifully gelatinous chunks out of trotters. To paraphrase an old Marlboro advert: Offal, Come to where the flavour (and texture) is.

All that swishing and swatting makes oxtail a wonderful cut of meat. Mooing with bovine heft, it has a spectacular depth of flavour. It's best slow-cooked, and this recipe is inspired by Paula Wolfert's wonderful The Cooking of South West France. *It takes time, two days to be precise, but despite a rather wordy recipe, it's not difficult to make.*

Oxtail Daube

SERVES 6

1 calf's foot, split (optional, but
    makes all the difference)
250g/9oz salt pork (if you
    can't get this, ask the
    butcher for a lump of
    unsliced streaky bacon)
2–3 tbsp sunflower oil
2–3kg/4½–6½lb oxtail, cut
    into rounds
sea salt and freshly ground
    black pepper
6 onions, roughly chopped
75cl bottle of punchy red wine
3 garlic cloves, peeled
bouquet garni (4 parsley
    stalks, 1 sprig of thyme,
    1 bay leaf, tied together)
handful of chopped parsley

Start making this two days before you want to eat it. Preheat the oven to fan 140°C/275°F/Gas 2. Put the calf's foot, if using, and salt pork in a pan with cold water to cover, bring to the boil and simmer for 5 minutes, then drain and reserve the calf's foot. If using salt pork, slice off the rind and set aside. Cut the pork or bacon into 3–4cm/1¼-inch cubes. Heat 1 tbsp oil in a large, heavy-bottomed frying pan and slowly brown the meat; you want to render away most of the fat and get a good golden tan.

Line a very large, heavy casserole with the salt pork rind, if using, fat side down. Add the pork or bacon cubes.

Brown the oxtail in the frying pan, in batches, adding more oil if necessary. Transfer to the casserole and put over a low heat, grinding in some pepper.

In the same frying pan, cook the onions until golden, adding a little more oil if necessary. Using a slotted spoon, add them to the casserole. Deglaze the frying pan with a glass of wine, and boil down to a thick glaze. Add the remaining wine, over a high heat, plus about 1 litre/1¾ pints water. Bring to the boil, and skim if necessary. Pour into the casserole, add the calf's foot, if using, the garlic and bouquet garni. Cover tightly and bake for 4 hours (or cook over a low heat on the hob). Do not touch it while it cooks. Leave the oven on.

Using a slotted spoon, remove the oxtails, set aside and cover. Pick the meat off the calf's foot and add to the oxtail. Strain the cooking liquid into a large bowl and leave to cool. Once cool, cover and put it in the fridge so the fat sets hard on top and becomes easier to remove.

Remove the fat from the cooking liquid, then pour the liquid into a wide pan and bring to the boil. Put the oxtail and calf's foot meat back in the now empty casserole, pour the hot liquid around the meat, and bake for 1½ hours at fan 140°C/275°F/Gas 2, without disturbing. Leave to cool and put in the fridge overnight.

The next day, turn the oven to its lowest setting. Remove any remaining fat from the surface of the casserole, then put the oxtail pieces into a baking dish in the oven at fan 160°C/325°F/Gas 4 until hot through. Strain the sauce into a pan, bring to the boil and simmer, half over the heat, skimming if necessary, until the sauce is thick and glistening and coats the back of a spoon. Pour over the meat, sprinkle with parsley and serve with mashed potatoes, or noodles and a crisp green salad.

I love cheek. All that work chewing the cud means that it has a proper flavour punch and, if treated with low heat and a bit of liquid, it'll break down into soft, silken strands. If you can't face a pie, then omit the pastry and serve as a stew, with mashed potatoes.

Braised Ox Cheek Pie

SERVES 4

2 ox cheeks (about 400g/14oz each) – ask your butcher to prepare these by removing the skin and fat – cut into 3–4cm/1¼-inch pieces

1 tbsp plain flour, plus extra for dusting

sea salt and freshly ground black pepper

2–3 tbsp vegetable oil

2 celery stalks, cut into chunky matchstick lengths

4 carrots, thickly sliced

200ml/7fl oz stout

1 litre/1¾ pints chicken stock (cube is fine)

2 tbsp Worcestershire sauce

1 bay leaf

2 leeks, sliced

350g/12oz all-butter puff pastry

1 egg, beaten

This can be cooked on the hob or in the oven; if the latter, preheat the oven to fan 150°C/300°F/Gas 3. Season the flour with salt and pepper and toss the ox cheek in the flour. Heat 1 tbsp oil in a frying pan and brown the meat in batches, adding a little more oil if necessary; set aside in a large, heavy casserole. Lightly brown the celery and carrots in the frying pan, adding 1 tbsp oil if needed, then put into the casserole.

Deglaze the frying pan with a little of the stout, stirring to loosen the browned bits, then pour over the beef and vegetables. Cover with the stock, the remaining stout and the Worcestershire sauce, add the bay leaf and bring to the boil, then cover and simmer gently – or transfer to the oven – for about 2 hours, until the meat is tender.

Remove the lid and cook for a further 30 minutes, adding the leeks for the final 10 minutes, until the sauce is thick. Put the mixture into a 1-litre/1¾-pint pie dish and place a pie funnel in the middle. Cover loosely and leave to cool.

Preheat the oven to fan 180°C/350°F/Gas 6. On a lightly floured surface, roll out the pastry until it is about 6cm/ 2½ inches larger than the size of the pie dish. Cut three 2cm/¾-inch wide strips from the end of the pastry. Brush the rim of the pie dish lightly with beaten egg and lay the strips around the rim. Brush the strips very lightly with more egg.

Cut a small cross, about 2cm/¾ inch wide, in the middle of the rolled-out pastry, then lay it over the filling, pressing down well around the rim of the dish to stick the pastry together. Using a sharp knife, trim any excess pastry from the edge of the pie, then knock up the edges of the pastry. Brush the top of the pie with beaten egg to glaze, taking care not to brush the knocked-up edges.

Bake for about 25 minutes, until the pastry is golden and the filling is bubbling. Serve hot.

'We miss a great deal through static loyalty to a stagecoach cuisine,' writes Victor Gordon in The English Cookbook, *before going on to bemoan our lack of culinary progress when compared to the French. But in this wonderful tome, published in 1985, he tries to 'start a process of renewal for English cooking and British culinary practice'. The book pretty much succeeds, bringing old recipes up to date. These instructions for oxtail are adapted from just one of its many beautiful recipes.*

A Summer's Tail

SERVES 6

1 x 1kg/2lb 4oz oxtail, cut into rounds
sea salt and freshly ground black pepper
1 tbsp sunflower oil
2 large onions, unpeeled, quartered
5 tbsp cider vinegar
2 litres/3½ pints fresh hot veal or beef stock (*see* page 227)
4 carrots, roughly chopped
1 bay leaf
4 sprigs of fresh thyme
1 tsp black peppercorns
large handful of fresh parsley, finely chopped
large handful of fresh chives, snipped
4 pickled walnuts, broken into pieces
2–6 leaves of gelatine, depending on the quality of your stock
glug of Worcestershire sauce (optional)
175ml/6fl oz port or Madeira
crusty bread, to serve

Put 2 litres/3½ pints well-salted water in a bowl, add the oxtail, cover and soak for 2 hours. Drain, rinse and put in a pan of unsalted water, bring to the boil and simmer for 15 minutes. Drain and pat dry. Preheat the oven to fan 200°C/400°F/ Gas 7.

Coat the oxtail in the oil, then put in a casserole and roast for 10 minutes. Shake the pan, add the onions and roast for 10 minutes. Add the vinegar and, when it has reduced, add the stock, carrots, bay, thyme and peppercorns. Turn the oven down to fan 160°C/325°F/Gas 4, cover the casserole and cook for 2½ hours, skimming a couple of times in the first 30 minutes if necessary. When the meat is falling off the bones, lift out the oxtail using a slotted spoon, cover and put in the fridge. Leave the liquid to simmer for 30 minutes, strain into a jug and, when cool, cover and put in the fridge for a few hours.

Remove the fat (it should now be hard) from the liquor and discard. The cold broth should be wobbling and jelly-like. If not, reduce it more: you should have 800ml/1½ pints.

Line six 200ml/7fl oz ramekins with clingfilm. Remove any fat from the oxtail, then pick off all the meat and put in a bowl with the parsley, chives and pickled walnuts. Mix evenly, then divide the mixture among the ramekins.

The broth needs to set to a firm jelly; how much gelatine you need depends on the thickness of your stock. Soak the gelatine in water for 5 minutes, until soft. Reheat the broth in a saucepan, adding salt, pepper, and Worcestershire sauce if using, to taste. Squeeze the water out of the gelatine, add the gelatine to the hot broth and stir until dissolved. Add the port and simmer for 2 minutes. Pour the broth, hot but not boiling, into the ramekins and leave for a few hours to cool and set. Turn out onto plates and serve with crusty bread.

Kidneys are so underrated, the best being lambs' and calves'. This is a tapas dish from Spain, and you need dry sherry here: fino or manzanilla.

Kidneys in Sherry

SERVES 4

400g/14oz lambs' or calves' kidneys, rinsed and patted dry

about 2 tbsp olive oil

1 onion, thinly sliced

2 garlic cloves, finely chopped

1 tbsp plain flour

sea salt and freshly ground black pepper

200ml/7fl oz fino or manzanilla sherry

squeeze of lemon juice

handful of fresh parsley, finely chopped

Cut lambs' kidneys in half and calves' kidneys into 5cm/2-inch chunks and snip out the the cores and gristle with scissors. Heat the oil in a frying pan and cook the onion and garlic for 15 minutes, until soft and lightly coloured.

Meanwhile, season the flour with salt and pepper, then roll the kidneys in the flour.

Turn up the heat under the pan and add the kidneys. Cook for 3 minutes, turning once or twice, then add the sherry and bubble it down for 2–3 minutes, scraping up the sediment from the bottom of the pan. Cook until the kidneys are just pink, then serve at once, with a squeeze of lemon on top and a scattering of chopped parsley.

Lady Maclean's Cookbook *is possibly the grandest collection of recipes you'll ever read. Either typed or handwritten, you'll find wonderfully old-fashioned recipes from duchesses (Devonshire and Argyll), Davids (well, Elizabeth David, pure gastronomic royalty) and endless Ladies. This kidney recipe is adapted from one by Diana, Countess of Westmorland, and is splendidly rich and rib-sticking.*

Very Grand Kidneys

Parboil the potatoes for about 12 minutes. Drain and leave to cool, then remove the skins and cut into small cubes.

To make the béchamel, put the milk in a pan and heat until it's just about to boil, then set aside. Melt the butter in a saucepan and stir in the flour over a medium heat, until you have a smooth, just golden roux. Gradually add the hot milk, stirring all the time (I use a mini-whisk with a horseshoe-shaped twist of wire at the end) until the sauce is thick and velvety smooth. When it comes to the boil, stop stirring and cook gently for about 10 minutes. Add salt and pepper to taste. Set aside. Preheat the oven to fan 170°C/340°F/Gas 5.

Cut the kidneys in half and snip out the cores and gristle with scissors, then chop the kidneys into small pieces. Heat 25g/1oz of the butter in a large frying pan over a medium–low heat and sauté the kidneys until just cooked, about 3–4 minutes. Season with salt and pepper, remove and set aside.

Remove the pan from the heat and wipe it out with kitchen paper. Add the remaining butter and gently cook the onions with the potatoes for 10–15 minutes, until the onions are soft and lightly browned.

Spoon the potatoes and onions into a buttered, shallow ovenproof dish, season with salt and pepper, then add the kidneys and pour over the warm béchamel sauce. Sprinkle with the Parmesan and bake for 20–25 minutes, until bubbling. Scatter over the parsley and serve with crusty bread.

SERVES 4

4 large floury potatoes
8 lambs' kidneys, rinsed and
    patted dry
75g/2¾ oz butter, plus extra
    for greasing
sea salt and freshly ground
    black pepper
2 large onions, thinly sliced
50g/1¾oz Parmesan, grated
handful of fresh parsley, finely
    chopped
crusty bread, to serve

BÉCHAMEL SAUCE
300ml/10fl oz full-fat milk
25g/1oz butter
25g/1oz plain flour
salt and freshly ground black
    pepper

Crisp pig's ears with a spicy hot sauce – a true pleasure.

Spiced Crisp Pig's Ears

SERVES 2

2 pig's ears, cleaned
1 onion, cut into quarters
1 carrot, roughly chopped
1 celery stalk, roughly
   chopped
2 dried chillies
1 star anise
1 cinnamon stick
150ml/5fl oz rice wine
5 black peppercorns
4 tbsp plain flour
sea salt
1 tbsp mustard powder
250ml/9fl oz vegetable oil

DIPPING SAUCE
50ml/2fl oz Thai fish sauce
150ml/5fl oz fresh lime juice
4 bird's-eye chillies, finely
   chopped

Cook the pig's ears in lightly salted boiling water for 3 minutes. Drain and set aside. Return them to the pan and add the vegetables, spices and rice wine. Cover with cold water, bring to the boil and simmer gently for 1½ hours. Drain and leave to cool, then slice very thinly down the ears.

Season the flour with salt and the mustard powder and put it on a plate. Dip the ears in the mixture, shaking away excess.

In a deep pan, heat the oil to 180°C/350°F, or until a cube of bread browns in 30 seconds. Deep-fry the ears in batches, until crisp. Drain on kitchen paper.

Mix together the ingredients for the dipping sauce and serve with the pig's ear crisps.

This was one of my mother's dinner party dishes, rich, boozy and sealed with a thin crust of butter. She used to make it the old-fashioned way, cooking raw livers gently in a bain-marie. She added a lot more cream than I use; I've reduced it, not for dreary health reasons (God forbid), but simply because I think it's unnecessary. A little smoked bacon adds porky depth. Serve on thin, crustless toast.

Chicken Liver Pâté

SERVES 4–6

150g/5½oz unsalted butter
3 shallots, finely chopped
2 garlic cloves, finely chopped
6 rashers of good smoked
    back bacon
500g/1lb 2oz chicken livers,
    trimmed
¼ tsp cayenne pepper
2–3 tbsp brandy, warmed
3 tbsp double cream
sea salt and freshly ground
    black pepper

Put half the butter in a frying pan over a medium heat. Add the shallots and garlic and cook until soft, about 10 minutes. Remove from the pan and set aside.

Add the bacon and cook until it begins to release its fat, then add the livers and cook, stirring from time to time, until just pink inside, about 3–4 minutes. Add the cayenne, then turn up the heat and whack in the brandy; it should ignite. After about 20 seconds, once the booze has burned off, tip the lot into a food processor, along with the shallots and garlic, and whizz until smooth. Stir in the cream and season well.

Decant into a shallow dish, or individual ramekins. Melt the remaining butter over a medium–low heat, then remove from the heat and leave to stand for a couple of minutes, until the milk solids sink to the bottom. Pour the clear butter over the pâté, leaving the milk solids behind. Cover and chill in the fridge for 2 hours. Serve with white toast, crusts cut off.

ALL about WILD MEAT

We live in a land awash and a-run with wild animals and game. From late summer through to the last dregs of winter, they're everywhere. Soaring over guns, gambolling down hills, thumping into cars. Yet many of us still see these wild beasts and birds as some form of extreme eating, fit only for bloodthirsty, swivel-eyed, thrill-seeking carnivores. The gustatorially deranged types who crave the stink of rotten flesh.

But a young grouse, quickly roasted and served in a pool of clear gravy, is one of the most sweet and delicate things that will ever pass your lips. It makes a pork chop seem positively coarse. The same goes for partridge. And pheasant, cooked properly, can delight.

It's not just the birds that make British game so great, but wild rabbit too, lean and hopping with flavour. And hare, that lithe and long-limbed beast, beloved of pagans and despised by Christian monks (hares were known as light-bearers to Eostre, the Celtic goddess of dawn, fertility and rebirth, so were made out to be sinister and steeped in the dark arts by those oh-so-pious monks). Hare can have a strong flavour, but it packs a magnificent punch. Once you have a taste for it, there's no going back.

As for venison ... contrary to popular belief, it isn't one species, rather a collection of species, all with their own separate charms. The majestic red deer, the wonderful roe, as well as muntjac, sika and Chinese water deer. The flavours vary, depending on the length of time the carcass has been hung. But a restaurateur friend introduced me to fallow deer tartare. It's sublime. Rich, subtle and seductive, it was the best raw meat I've ever eaten.

OK, so woodcock and snipe might not be to all tastes. The former is traditionally served with head and long, elegant beak still attached. And the skull should be hewn open to reveal the silken brains. But these are wild meats with charm and depth and endless allure. And the fact that most (save rabbit) have a legally defined season means that when they are about, we appreciate them all the more.

This came about when I was asked to rustle up some Christmas canapés for a corporate gig. I have little time for traditional Christmas food (yawn) and even less for those insubstantial mouthfuls that never quite satisfy, so I prefer this as a first course. The likes of juniper and allspice work wonders with venison, especially when raw. Chop the meat by hand, having ensured that every last trace of fat and sinew is removed.

Spiced Venison Tartare

SERVES 4

300g/10½oz venison fillet, trimmed of excess fat, very finely chopped

2 tbsp capers, rinsed and very finely chopped

6 cornichons, very finely chopped

1 shallot, very finely chopped

6 juniper berries, crushed and very finely chopped

3 allspice berries, crushed and very finely chopped

4 sprigs of fresh thyme, leaves removed and very finely chopped

½ tsp ground white pepper

½ tsp ground cinnamon

sea salt and freshly ground black pepper

2 tsp Dijon mustard, or to taste

big jig of Worcestershire sauce

good jig of Tabasco

4 egg yolks

4 square pieces of sourdough toast

Gently mix the venison with the capers, cornichons, shallot, juniper, allspice, thyme, white pepper, cinnamon and a good grinding of black pepper. Taste and add salt.

Add the mustard, Worcestershire sauce and Tabasco. Mix gently and taste, adding more mustard or sauce if you like: the mixture should have punch but no flavour should dominate.

Shape into four neat patties and put on plates. Make a small hollow in the top of each, top with a raw egg yolk and serve with sourdough toast.

I first tried this in Lipari, in the Aeolian Islands, to the north of Sicily. It was made using wild rabbit from the nearby island of Filicudi. I've only set foot on this wild and remote place once. We sailed over from Lipari in my friend Luca's small boat, then hired scooters to get us up into the hills. I remember baked ricotta, stunning tomatoes and a rather wild party that went on well into the next day. The journey back was rather more painful, although frequent stops for swims in the brilliantly azure sea made things a little more bearable. If you can use wild rabbit, do. The flavour's better. If not, go farmed.

Aeolian Rabbit with Potatoes

SERVES 4

2 wild rabbits, each jointed
  into 6 pieces
1 lemon, halved, plus the juice
  of 1 lemon
4 bay leaves
400g/14oz small waxy
  potatoes, halved, or
  quartered if large
sea salt and freshly ground
  black pepper
4 tbsp olive oil
3 garlic cloves, roughly
  chopped
3 fresh rosemary stalks
2 tbsp capers, rinsed
100g/3½oz green olives
100ml/3½fl oz white wine
  vinegar

Put the rabbit pieces, lemon halves and 2 bay leaves in a large saucepan and cover with cold water. Bring to a simmer and cook over a gentle heat for 2 hours, or until completely tender (farmed rabbits will take less time).

About 20 minutes before the rabbit is ready, cook the potatoes in a pan of lightly salted boiling water for 15 minutes, or until tender; drain. Heat 2 tbsp oil in a frying pan and cook the potatoes over a medium–high heat until crisp and brown, turning regularly.

Transfer the rabbit pieces to a plate using a slotted spoon (reserve the stock for a soup). Heat the remaining oil in a heavy-bottomed pot over a medium–high heat, add the rabbit and cook for 3–4 minutes, turning once or twice, until lightly browned. Add the garlic, rosemary, capers, olives and remaining bay leaves, and season with salt and pepper. Cook for 2 minutes, stirring and making sure nothing burns. Add the vinegar and allow to cook off.

Reduce the heat, add the potatoes and stir gently. Add the lemon juice and leave for a few minutes, stir, then serve.

Agrodolce ('sour-sweet') is a particularly Sicilian taste, introduced by the Moors. Its most famous incarnation is caponata, a wonderfully sweet-and-sour mix of aubergine, celery and capers, with endless regional variations. Like the recipe on page 176, this is from the Aeolian Islands, off the north coast of Sicily, where it's made with wild rabbits: they are smaller but have more flavour than the plumper and more mild-flavoured farmed rabbits.

Coniglio in Agrodolce

Put the rabbit pieces, halved onion, lemon zest and bay leaves in a large saucepan and cover with 2 litres/3½ pints cold water. Bring to a simmer and cook over a gentle heat for about 1½ hours, turning halfway through (if using farmed rabbits, cook for about 1 hour).

Transfer the rabbit pieces to a plate using a slotted spoon and pat dry with kitchen paper. Strain the stock and reserve (you should have around 500ml/18fl oz).

Heat 2 tbsp of the oil in a large frying pan over a medium–high heat. Add the rabbit, cook until browned on all sides, then transfer to a wide casserole. Add the remaining oil to the frying pan and gently cook the sliced onions for about 10 minutes, until softened and lightly golden, adding the garlic for the final 2 minutes of cooking. Tip the onions and garlic into the casserole with the rabbit.

Turn up the heat under the frying pan and add the Marsala, stirring to deglaze. Add the tomatoes and 200ml/7fl oz of the reserved rabbit stock.

Bring to a simmer, then pour over the rabbit and onions. Stir in a further 200ml/7fl oz of rabbit stock, cover the pan with a lid, and cook over a gentle heat for 45 minutes, or until the rabbit is tender. Check every 15 minutes or so, and add more stock if the sauce needs to be loosened.

Remove the lid and cook for a further 15 minutes, or until the sauce has thickened and the rabbit is very tender. Season with salt and pepper to taste, transfer to a serving dish and sprinkle with the almonds.

SERVES 4

2 wild rabbits, each jointed into 6 pieces

3 onions, 1 halved and 2 thinly sliced

2 long strips of peel from an unwaxed lemon

2 bay leaves

4 tbsp olive oil

2 garlic cloves, crushed

150ml/5fl oz Marsala

2 x 400g/14oz cans of chopped tomatoes

sea salt and freshly ground black pepper

25g/1oz flaked almonds, lightly toasted

This is one of my step-father's favourite dishes, and any game can be used. Grouse is my favourite, but partridge works well, as does woodcock or snipe. Visun, my step-father's former head chef, is a talented man. I love the way he layers game birds in risotto. This sort of classical food takes elbow grease. It is, though, time well spent. You could use two partridges, three woodcocks or snipe, or a small free-range chicken instead of grouse, but would need to adjust the cooking time.

Game Pudding

SERVES 4

2 tbsp olive oil

2 grouse

1 carrot, diced

1 celery stalk, diced

1 leek, white part only, diced

1 shallot, halved

1 bay leaf

1 sprig of fresh thyme

1 sprig of fresh rosemary

3 juniper berries

100ml/3½fl oz red wine

300ml/10fl oz fresh dark chicken stock (*see* page 226)

25g/1oz butter, plus extra for greasing

sea salt and freshly ground black pepper

RISOTTO

1 tbsp olive oil

250g/9oz arborio rice

100ml/3½fl oz red wine

100ml/3½fl oz port

1 litre/1¾ pints hot fresh dark chicken stock (*see* page 226)

50g/1¾oz cooked fresh peas or frozen peas

50g/1¾oz Parmesan, finely grated

1 tsp mascarpone

1 tsp unsalted butter

Preheat the oven to fan 150°C/300°F/Gas 3. Heat the oil in a roasting tin and brown the grouse and vegetables over a medium–high heat. Add the bay leaf, thyme, rosemary and juniper berries and deglaze with the wine. When the wine has reduced, add the stock. Cover tightly with foil and transfer to the oven; cook for 1 hour, or until the grouse are cooked; this will depend on their age and size.

While the game is braising, make the risotto: heat the oil in a saucepan, add the rice and toast over a medium heat for 4 minutes, stirring with a wooden spoon. Add the red wine and stir; when it has been absorbed, add the port and stir again. When the port is reduced, add 150ml/5fl oz of hot chicken stock, stir once, then leave until the rice has absorbed the stock before adding more; continue until all the stock is used up – the risotto must be slightly dry. Add the peas, stir for a minute, then take off the heat and add the Parmesan, mascarpone and butter. Beat with a wooden spoon. Spread the risotto evenly on a clingfilm-lined baking tray and leave to cool.

Leave the braised birds to cool, then discard the skin, remove the meat and break into large 'threads'. Strain the cooking liquid through a sieve and discard the vegetables. Add 3 tbsp of the cooking liquid to the meat, stir well, cover and set aside.

To make the red wine sauce, put the wine, Marsala and juniper in a pan and boil to reduce by half. Add the game stock and simmer until the sauce reduces enough to coat the back of a spoon. Strain through a sieve and set aside.

To assemble, butter a 1.2-litre/2-pint pudding bowl and place a disc of baking parchment in the bottom. Start with a layer of cold risotto, about 2cm/¾ inch thick, then add a layer of the shredded game and dot 1 tsp butter over the meat, seasoning as you go. Repeat this process until you use all the game and rice, finishing with a layer of rice. Cover the bowl with a layer of baking parchment and then a layer of foil. Secure the foil tightly around the edge of the bowl and tie firmly with string. Create a handle with the string to enable you to lift the bowl out of the pan.

Place a small upturned heatproof plate or trivet in the bottom of a large pan and lower in the pudding bowl. Carefully pour in enough boiling water to come about one-third of the way up the sides of the bowl. Cover the pan with a lid and simmer for 1 hour, checking every now and again that it isn't boiling dry.

Turn out the pudding and drizzle with the red wine sauce. Serve with steamed vegetables.

RED WINE SAUCE
½ bottle (37.5cl) red wine
175ml/6fl oz Marsala
6 juniper berries, crushed
600ml/20fl oz fresh game
  stock (*see* page 224)
300ml/10fl oz veal or beef
  stock (*see* page 227)

This sounds fiddly, but it's a wonderful way to use game. I often cook charity dinners with my friend Matthew Fort, and he reckons they want something more, well, sophisticated, than my usual fare. This works beautifully. The key is to under-cook the birds at the start, as there's a further cooking process. It's long-winded, fairly classical French cooking. But worth the effort.

Game Salmi

SERVES 6

2 pheasants, or 3 partridges, or a mixture of both, or use guinea fowl or grouse – you want all the bits, from neck to gizzard, if possible

2 tbsp olive oil

sea salt and freshly ground black pepper

2 celery stalks, roughly chopped

2 large carrots, roughly chopped

2 onions, roughly chopped

2 tomatoes, deseeded and roughly chopped

2 bay leaves

fistful of fresh thyme sprigs

4 juniper berries

250ml/9fl oz dry white wine

24 chestnuts, or 200g/7oz vacuum-packed cooked chestnuts

40g/1½oz butter

40g/1½oz plain flour

2 tbsp double cream

handful of fresh flat-leaf parsley, roughly chopped

Preheat the oven to fan 180°C/350°F/Gas 6. Rub the birds with 1 tbsp oil and season lightly.

Put the celery, carrots, onions and tomatoes in a roasting tin, add a glug of oil and put the birds on top, with any giblets (except the liver). Roast for 20 minutes, until the skins turn brown. Remove the birds and leave to cool. Put the tray back in the oven and roast the vegetables for a further 20 minutes.

Meanwhile, joint the birds: push each leg away from the body and cut off. Slice off the breasts, in one piece if possible. They should be quite undercooked. Cover and chill until required.

Rip apart the carcasses and place, with the skin and any giblets, in a large pot along with the roasted vegetables, the bay leaves, thyme and juniper. Cover with 1.5 litres/2½ pints cold water and bring to the boil.

Meanwhile, pour off any excess fat from the roasting tin, place over a medium–high heat and deglaze with the white wine. Pour into the stock pot. Once it is boiling, skim and reduce the heat to a medium simmer; bubble for about 2 hours.

If using raw chestnuts in their shells, turn the oven up to fan 220°C/425°F/Gas 9. Score the shells and roast the chestnuts until charred. Set aside until cool enough to handle, then peel. Cut the roasted or vacuum-packed chestnuts into small chunks.

When the stock is ready, strain through a fine sieve. If you can, strain again through muslin. It should taste rich and nicely gamy. If too weak, boil it down by a third and taste again.

Melt the butter in a heavy-bottomed pan, then add the flour, stirring constantly. Gradually add 600ml/20fl oz of the stock, stirring, and simmer for 5 minutes, until thickened. Season to taste. Add the chestnuts, game and cream, and warm through for 2–3 minutes. Scatter with the parsley and serve with buttered Savoy cabbage and mashed potatoes.

This is from my great friend Matthew Fort, a wonderful food writer and world-class trencherman. He happily admits it was inspired by a recipe for duck ham in Michel Guérard's Cuisine Gourmande *(1978). Come late autumn and into winter, there's a glut of pheasant. And this recipe is beautiful. Simply cut off the breasts, and use the rest of the body for stock (see page 224). This recipe is for eight breasts, although as Matthew says, 'you can do them in any number, one to one hundred. If you're going to use a load of salt every time you make pheasant ham, you might as well get a few done at the same time. There's no need to go fancy with the salt. It makes no difference to the curing what you use. Therefore, the cheaper the better.'*

Matthew's Pheasant Ham

SERVES 8

1 tsp coriander seeds
1 tsp allspice berries
1 tsp juniper berries
2 tsp black peppercorns
½ star anise
4 bay leaves
about 1kg/2lb 4oz salt
8 pheasant breasts, skinned

Thoroughly crush all the spices in a mortar. Chop up the bay leaves quite finely.

On a non-reactive tray or a ceramic or glass dish, spread a good layer of salt, about 5mm/¼ inch thick. Sprinkle half the crushed spices and bay leaf over the salt, then lay the pheasant breasts on top. Sprinkle the remaining spices over the breasts and then cover with the remaining salt. The breasts must be well covered, looking like hills with a good fall of snow on them. Cover and leave in the fridge for 24–36 hours.

Rinse off the salt very thoroughly, but try to leave some of the crushed spices sticking to the breasts. Dry thoroughly.

The hams are now ready to use; or wrap them in clingfilm and freeze for up to 1 month. Slice thinly.

A classic Anglo-Indian dish. I first tried this at Gymkhana, an exceptionally good regional Indian place in Mayfair. The meat was soft, but not pappy, the pepper punchy but not overwhelming. It was redolent of bangles and bungalows, gurus, khaki, tiffin and teak. You can use eight boneless chicken thighs instead of the partridge, but you will need to adjust the simmering time.

Partridge Pepper Fry

Cut the legs and breasts off the partridge and set aside. (Keep the carcass for stock, *see* page 224.)

Heat the oil in a large, heavy pan over a medium heat. Add the whole spices and cook until they become fragrant and begin to pop. Add the onion, chillies, ginger and garlic and cook until soft.

Add the turmeric and chilli powder, and most of the ground black pepper. Cook for a minute, then whack up the heat and add the meat. Season with salt, then cook over a high heat for a few minutes to brown the meat.

Add a dash of water, cover and simmer gently for about 10 minutes. Remove the lid and reduce over a high heat for 3–5 minutes, stirring regularly, until just dry.

Add the rest of ground pepper and the garam masala, cook for another minute, and finish with the sliced chilli, ginger, a good squeeze of lemon juice and the curry leaves. Serve with rice or naan bread.

SERVES 4

4 whole partridge, or
   8 boneless chicken thighs
4 tbsp groundnut or vegetable
   oil
½ cinnamon stick
2 cloves
2 green cardamom pods
8 black peppercorns
1 tsp black mustard seeds
1 tsp coriander seeds
4 curry leaves
1 large onion, finely chopped
3 green finger chillies, split
   lengthwise
5cm/2-inch piece of fresh
   ginger, peeled and finely
   grated, plus extra to serve,
   thinly sliced
2 garlic cloves, very thinly
   sliced
¼ tsp ground turmeric
½ tsp chilli powder
1 tbsp ground black pepper
sea salt
1 tsp garam masala (*see* page
   222)
1 green chilli, finely chopped
juice of ½ lemon
5 curry leaves

This is High Church Italian cooking, fairly elaborate and not without a touch of the Gallic. In fact, the 'bombas di riso' you find in Naples are very much descended from the French court. This bomba, made with pigeons, hails from Piacenza in Emilia, and can get truly decadent, studded with great chunks of white truffles and soft nuggets of sweetbread. This is a fairly simple version. Fiddle as much as you desire.

A Pigeon Bomba from Emilia-Romagna

SERVES 4

75g/2¾oz butter, plus extra for greasing

1 tbsp olive oil

4 pigeons

2 onions, 1 roughly chopped and 1 finely chopped

1 carrot, roughly chopped

1 celery stalk, roughly chopped

1 tomato, quartered

250ml/9fl oz dry white wine

2 tbsp tomato purée

6 peppercorns

2 bay leaves

400g/14oz arborio rice

1 litre/1¾ pints fresh light chicken stock, boiling (*see* page 223)

150g/5½oz frozen peas

250g/9oz Parmesan, finely grated

sea salt and freshly ground black pepper

25g/1oz fine dry white breadcrumbs

Heat 25g/1oz of the butter with the oil in a wide, deep pan and brown the birds to a good dark colour. Remove and set aside. In the same pan, brown the roughly chopped onion, carrot, celery and tomato. Deglaze with the white wine, stirring to loosen the browned bits, then add the tomato purée and simmer to reduce slightly.

Put the pigeons back in the pan, add the peppercorns, bay leaves and water to cover and simmer for 1–1¼ hours, until the pigeons are cooked. Transfer the birds to a board until cool enough to handle and then remove the meat and set aside. Return the bones to the broth and simmer for another hour. Strain the broth and reserve.

In another heavy pan, melt the remaining butter over a low heat and cook the finely chopped onion until completely soft. Add the rice, stirring until it is well coated in butter. Add the hot stock and simmer gently for about 10–12 minutes, until the rice is just done, but still al dente. Add 400ml/14fl oz of the reserved pigeon stock, plus the peas and Parmesan, salt and pepper. Leave to stand for 20 minutes.

Preheat the oven to fan 180°C/350°F/Gas 6. Line a 23cm/9-inch springform tin with a disc of baking parchment and butter the base and sides generously. Sprinkle with the breadcrumbs and roll around the inside of the tin to coat lightly. Add a layer of the rice mixture, then a thin layer of pigeon meat, then rice, then pigeon, until all is used, finishing with a layer of rice. Cover tightly with foil, place on a large baking sheet and bake for 1 hour. Loosen the sides with a round-bladed knife, turn out and serve.

Good Things in England *(1932) is one of the great works on English food, a compendium of recipes drawn from across the country; 'an attempt', in the words of its author Florence White, 'to capture the charm of England's cookery before it is completely crushed out of existence'. She was a rather tragic, lonely figure, but her book stands the testament of time. This recipe is inspired by a dish in the book, and manages to be both rich and fresh.*

Duck and Peas

Preheat the oven to fan 200°C/400°F/Gas 7. Season inside the duck with salt and pepper, then put in the orange and half of the onion. Massage the duck with oil, season and roast for 30 minutes, until lightly browned.

Transfer the duck to a heavy casserole, breast side up, and add the stock along with the sage, mint, allspice, orange peel and the remaining onion. Cover the pan and simmer over a low heat for about 1½ hours, until tender.

Remove the duck and set aside. Add the port to the casserole and reduce the sauce over a high heat for around 5 minutes, until slightly thickened – it should very lightly coat the back of a spoon. Add the peas and cook for 2 minutes.

Remove the orange peel, then season the sauce with salt and pepper to taste. Pour the sauce around the duck on a large serving plate. Serve with mashed potatoes.

SERVES 4

1 x 1.8kg/4lb duck, ready for roasting
sea salt and freshly ground black pepper
1 orange, quartered
1 onion, thinly sliced
1 tbsp sunflower oil
600ml/20fl oz fresh beef stock (*see* page 227)
4 fresh sage leaves
2 tsp finely chopped fresh mint
3 allspice berries, crushed
1 long strip of orange peel
250ml/9fl oz port
400g/14oz frozen peas

No
MEAT

ALL about

no

MEAT

So here we are. In a book about meat, starting a chapter that contains no meat. Not a jot. Not even a splash of stock, or soupçon of soused pig. But good food is about flavour, and I'm equally happy eating beautifully spiced lentils or a proper tomato sauce as I am attacking a rack of slow-smoked ribs.

The older I get, the more sense I see in vegetables. And pulses and legumes and all the rest. Joy too. Many years ago, I delighted in abusing vegetarians for their lily-livered, yogurt-eating ways. What a wit. But I also thought that Jim Morrison was a finer poet than Keats. Which says it all. You grow up, get wiser (hopefully) and less judgemental. I don't think I'll ever turn fully vegetarian, but a couple of days a week makes perfect sense. Not as some self-flagellating exercise in restraint, more straightforward, edible common sense.

A pasta pomodoro here, avocado and lime on toast there; vibrant vegetable curry (*see* pages 194 and 200), raw peas and broad beans by the pound (it's early summer as I write this). Plus asparagus dripping with butter, soft-boiled gulls' eggs and Sichuan smacked cucumber salad (*see* page 205). With dishes like these (well, in the case of the legumes, not even dishes), I don't miss flesh at all.

But this is a book called *Let's Eat Meat*. And although the likes of leeks vinaigrette (*see* page 197), frittelle di zucchini (*see* page 202) and TLS nachos (*see* page 207) are grand on their own, they also work wonderfully with many of the recipes in this book. I'm not suggesting you should splash Carolina red barbecue sauce (*see* page 215) on your green chicken curry, nor mix aloo dum (*see* page 194) with Neapolitan ragù (*see* page 76). But just as the dishes from the previous chapters come from across the globe, so do these meat-free beauties.

They add balance to the table, and contrast, crunch, charm and chew. Britain is one of the few countries where the diner is given his own individual portion, his and his alone. In China or Thailand, India or Mexico, food is about great dishes and plates to share. Food as communal activity, a bringer-together of folk, the great binder of civilisation. I love these recipes as much as every other in the book. They may not contain meat. But given that we're trying to eat less, but better, the chapter seems a fitting adieu.

Deep-fried risotto balls with a filling of either oozing mozzarella or slow-cooked meat ragù. When in Italy I find it very difficult to stroll past any street vendor or café without buying at least one. They're a southern Italian classic, and the Sicilian versions are usually larger than their Neapolitan cousins. The best I've ever tried were from a stall outside the main café in Marina Corta on Lipari, my favourite of the Aeolian Islands. They're pretty easy to make too. Either start from scratch, as I've done in this recipe, or use leftover risotto. I like them small: two-biters rather than great, hulking cannon balls.

Arancini di Riso

First make the tomato sauce: heat the oil in a pan, add the onion and cook for 10 minutes, until soft. Add the tomatoes, season with salt and pepper and cook gently for 40 minutes, stirring regularly. Add the basil leaves just before serving.

Cook the rice in a pan of salted boiling water for 16–18 minutes, or until very tender. Drain in a sieve, then tip into a bowl and leave to cool for 30 minutes.

Stir in the egg, then add the tomato purée and Parmesan and season generously.

Tip the breadcrumbs into a shallow bowl. Divide the rice mixture into 12 portions, but set aside about 3 tbsp. Roll each portion into a 4cm/1½-inch ball. Taking one ball at a time, hold it in the palm of one hand and make a dent in the middle, then either push a piece of mozzarella into the hollow, or add a generous teaspoon of the ragù. Cover the filling with a little of the reserved rice mixture, moulding gently to seal in the filling. Gently roll each ball in the breadcrumbs to coat, then set aside while you fill and coat the remaining *arancini*.

Heat the oil in a deep pan to about 170°C/340°F, or until a cube of bread turns golden in 30 seconds; alternatively, use an electric deep-fryer. Deep-fry the rice balls, four to six at a time, for about 5 minutes, until golden. Drain on kitchen paper and keep warm in a low oven while you cook the rest. Serve with the tomato sauce.

MAKES 12

125g/4½oz arborio rice
sea salt and freshly ground
    black pepper
1 large egg, lightly beaten
2 tbsp tomato purée
75g/2¾oz Parmesan, finely
    grated
50g/1¾oz fine dried
    breadcrumbs
1 ball of mozzarella, cut
    into 12 cubes, or 6 tbsp
    Neapolitan ragù (*see*
    page 76)
vegetable oil, for deep-frying

TOMATO SAUCE
1 tbsp olive oil
1 onion, finely chopped
2 x 400g/14oz cans of
    chopped tomatoes
a few leaves of basil, torn

An all-purpose Indian vegetable curry, this has many guises and variations. Peas and fried potatoes are classic ingredients, along with chillies and various herbs and spices. Eat as a side dish with partridge pepper fry (see page 185), chicken Lahori (see page 106) or any other curry dish.

Aloo Dum

SERVES 4

4 large floury potatoes, such as King Edward or Russet, peed and cut into 2cm/ ¾-inch cubes
vegetable or groundnut oil
1½ tsp ground turmeric
2 bay leaves
¼ tsp asafoetida
1 onion, roughly chopped
4 garlic cloves, finely chopped
2.5cm/1-inch piece of fresh ginger, peeled and finely grated
1 tsp chilli powder (Kashmiri if possible)
2 tsp ground coriander
2 tsp cumin seeds, toasted and ground
big pinch of salt
400g/14oz canned chopped tomatoes
4 green finger chillies, stalks removed, sliced into long strips
100g/3½oz frozen peas
1 tsp garam masala (*see* page 222)
handful of coriander leaves, chopped, to serve

Boil the potatoes in salted water for 6–8 minutes, until just about cooked, then drain.

Heat 3 tbsp oil in a heavy-bottomed saucepan and fry the potatoes for about 12 minutes, or until golden. Add 1 tsp of the turmeric and cook for another few minutes, then remove the potatoes with a slotted spoon and drain on kitchen paper.

Add another 1–2 tbsp oil to the pan over a medium heat, add the bay leaves and fry until they crackle, about 30 seconds. Add the asafoetida and stir, then add the onion and cook until soft, about 5 minutes. Add the garlic and ginger and cook for 1 minute, then add the chilli powder, ground coriander and cumin seeds, salt and the remaining turmeric and fry for another few minutes. Add the tomatoes, chillies and 150ml/5fl oz water and cook for 10 minutes. If it seems too thick, add a splash more water.

Reduce the heat, add the fried potatoes and cook for another 2 minutes, until hot, stirring occasionally. Add the peas and garam masala and cook for another 3 minutes, stirring regularly. To serve, throw over the chopped coriander.

This recipe for glazed onions is typically English. Unshowy, easy to make, and the perfect partner to a steak, roast leg of lamb or roast beef.

Glazed Onions

SERVES 4 AS A SIDE DISH

50g/1¾oz butter

450g/1lb silverskin (or pickling) onions, peeled and trimmed

½ tsp caster sugar

about 200ml/7fl oz fresh dark chicken or beef stock (*see* pages 226–227)

sea salt and freshly ground black pepper

Melt the butter in a wide, heavy-bottomed pan and when hot, add the onions and sprinkle with the sugar. Cover and cook over a low heat, shaking occasionally, for 10 minutes; they should be lightly coloured.

Add enough stock to cover the onions, put the lid back on, then cook for another 10 minutes or so, until the liquid has reduced to a glaze. Season to taste and serve hot.

I love this dish, so simple and clean and elegant, far more than the mere sum of its parts. The key is the marriage of vinaigrette and hard-boiled eggs, both sharp and soothing. And it is served at just above room temperature. Serve as a starter, or with a roast or with salad.

Leeks Vinaigrette

Chop off the roots and tops of the leeks, then wash under the cold tap until all the grit is gone.

Simmer in salted boiling water for about 6–7 minutes, depending on thickness, until on the brink of being tender. Remove and drain well.

Whisk together the vinegar, mustard, salt and pepper. Whisking constantly, very gradually pour in the oil until emulsified. Add the chopped yolks and whites and the parsley. Pour over the leeks and serve.

SERVES 4 AS A STARTER

8 sylph-like young leeks
1 tbsp white wine vinegar
1 tbsp Dijon mustard
sea salt and freshly ground
    black pepper
100ml/3½fl oz extra virgin
    olive oil
2 large hard-boiled eggs,
    peeled, yolks and whites
    chopped separately
handful of fresh parsley,
    roughly chopped

If you go to South Beach in Miami, you have to go to Joe's Stone Crab. It's open only in stone crab season (mid-October to mid-May), it takes hours to be seated (there's no booking) and prices are pretty high. But dear god, those stone crab claws, served with a mustard sauce, are sublime, with dense, pure white meat. 'Selects' are the best size, neither too big nor too small. And must be accompanied by a bowl of creamed spinach. Oh, and fried green tomatoes too, followed by Key lime pie. This is my version of the recipe: it's good with lamb, sausages or steaks.

Joe's Creamed Spinach

SERVES 4 AS A SIDE DISH

50g/1¾oz butter

500g/1lb 2oz spinach, thick stems removed and leaves finely shredded

300m/10fl oz double cream

a grating of nutmeg

big pinch of salt

Melt the butter, add the spinach and cook, stirring, until it wilts, 3–4 minutes.

Add the cream, nutmeg and salt and simmer for 3–4 minutes, until the cream is bubbling and slightly reduced. If you like, blitz briefly with a handheld blender to give a creamier texture. Serve hot.

This recipe is adapted from Arabella Boxer's Book of English Food, *one of my favourite cookbooks of all time. The recipe is typical of the book, grand but never snobby, elegant but understated. These tomatoes make a good match with cold roast beef (and for once, you do want the tomatoes fridge cold), and are great crammed in a sandwich with anything cold and meaty.*

Iced Tomatoes with Horseradish Sauce

Put the tomatoes in a bowl, pour boiling water over them and leave for a minute, then plunge into cold water and slip off the skins. Put the tomatoes in the fridge for a few hours.

Mix together the horseradish, crème fraîche and vinegar; chill.

To serve, slice the tomatoes, pour the sauce over and season with salt and pepper.

SERVES 4 AS A SIDE DISH

500g/1lb 2oz small, ripe tomatoes
sea salt and freshly ground black pepper

HORSERADISH SAUCE
20g/¾oz chunk of fresh horseradish, peeled and finely grated
5 tbsp crème fraîche
1 tsp white wine vinegar

You'll find this all over India — fiery and coconut spiked in the south, a little drier in Rajasthan and Gujarat. This is based on a Punjabi recipe, although I've added onion. Serve with a curry.

Chana Masala

SERVES 4

250g/9oz dried chickpeas, soaked in cold water overnight, rinsed and drained or 2 x 400g/14oz cans chickpeas, drained

3 tbsp sunflower oil

1 large onion, chopped

salt

1 tsp garam masala (*see* page 222)

juice of ½ lemon

handful of coriander leaves, to serve

MASALA PASTE

6 tomatoes, chopped

3 long green chillies, chopped

2 tsp chilli powder (Kashmiri if possible)

2 tbsp coriander seeds, lightly toasted

2 tsp ground cumin

2.5cm/1-inch piece of fresh ginger, peeled

6 garlic cloves, peeled

If using dried chickpeas, put them in a pan of water and bring to the boil. Boil for 10 minutes, then simmer for 50 minutes, until firm but soft.

To make the masala paste, blitz the tomatoes, fresh chillies, chilli powder, coriander seeds, cumin, ginger and garlic to a smooth paste.

Heat 1 tbsp oil in a large pan, add the onion and cook for about 20 minutes, until soft. Add 2 tbsp oil and fry the masala paste for about 5 minutes, stirring, until fragrant and cooked. Add 2 big pinches of salt.

Add the chickpeas and 300ml/10fl oz water, bring to the boil then simmer gently for about 15 minutes, stirring often. Stir in the garam masala and cook for another minute. Add the lemon juice and serve, scattered with coriander leaves.

Courgettes move me little. Sure, their flowers are good stuffed and deep-fried, in the Italian style. And in the Acapulco market I've eaten courgettes stuffed between masses of fresh white cheese and chile verde, and cooked in a quesadilla. But really, they don't turn me on. Fry them up in fritters, though, and they're a whole different prospect. Eat as a snack or starter.

Fritelle di Zucchini

SERVES 4 (MAKES 12 FRITTERS)

4 courgettes
3 large eggs
25g/1oz pecorino cheese, finely grated
1 tbsp chopped fresh parsley
sea salt and freshly ground black pepper
7 tbsp fine dry white breadcrumbs
2 spring onions, finely sliced diagonally, white and pale green parts only
vegetable oil for deep-frying
1 lemon, halved

Coarsely grate the courgettes, then squeeze to remove excess moisture and lay out on kitchen paper to drain for 10 minutes.

Whisk the eggs gently with the pecorino, parsley, salt, pepper and breadcrumbs.

Stir in the courgettes, spring onions, and more breadcrumbs, if need be, until you have a thickish, but flowing, batter.

Pour 2.5cm/1-inch oil into a wide, deep pan and heat until it's just shimmering. When you add a drop of the batter it should sizzle, then rise to the top in 30 seconds, crisp and golden.

Cook about four fritters at a time, dropping generously filled tablespoons of the mixture into the hot oil. Push them down with the back of a spoon to flatten, and cook for 1–2 minutes on each side.

Drain on kitchen paper and eat immediately, with a squeeze of lemon juice.

As a child, I used to dread coleslaw, a turgid, sullen mass of shredded whatever, all drowned in a cheap mayonnaise glop. Yuk. This version is pert, sharp and spiky, a perfect combination of crunch and vinegary vim. It cuts a dashing swathe through fat and stodge. It is good with ham and egg burgers (see page 43).

A Crisp, Sharp Coleslaw

Mix the cabbage, carrots and spring onions in a large bowl. In a small bowl, whisk together the vinegar, mustards, garlic and chilli. Dribble in the oil and whisk until emulsified. Pour the dressing over the vegetables and stir gently to coat; season with salt and pepper to taste. Leave in the fridge for an hour or two. Drain off any excess moisture before serving.

SERVES 6 AS A SIDE DISH

550g/1lb 2oz white cabbage, cored and shredded
2 large carrots, coarsely grated
10 spring onions, finely chopped
2 tbsp white wine vinegar
1 tbsp English mustard
1 tbsp Dijon mustard
2 garlic cloves, finely chopped
1 long green or jalapeño chilli, finely chopped
6 tbsp olive oil
sea salt and freshly ground black pepper

This dish combines the cool with the tongue-numbing and faintly hot. It makes a wonderful side dish with Sichuan boiled beef (see page 30).

Sichuan Smacked Cucumber Salad

Lightly bash the cucumbers with the flat side of a knife and then cut into 5cm/2-inch-long batons. Sprinkle the salt over the cucumbers and leave for 10 minutes. Pour away any liquid that has been drawn out.

Add the remaining ingredients and stir gently. Taste: it should be slightly sharp, numbing and a little spicy. If necessary, add an extra pinch of chilli or a few more peppercorns. Leave in the fridge for at least 30 minutes before serving.

SERVES 4 AS A SIDE DISH

2 cucumbers, peeled and
  deseeded
½ tsp fine sea salt
3 garlic cloves, finely chopped
2 tbsp soy sauce
½ tbsp sesame oil
1 tsp rice wine vinegar
pinch of caster sugar
1 tsp Sichuan peppercorns,
  ground
½ tsp dried chilli flakes

This is a weekly mainstay, and perfect whacked onto homemade kebabs, stirred into soups or thrown across tortillas. The key is a little heat (you can increase or decrease to taste) and a good whack of vinegar. Leave to stand for at least an hour for full flavour.

All-Purpose Salsa Crudo

SERVES 6–8

4 large tomatoes, deseeded
   and roughly chopped
1 cucumber, deseeded and cut
   into chunky cubes
1 large red onion, finely
   chopped
handful of fresh parsley, finely
   chopped
1–4 fresh chillies, finely
   chopped
2 tbsp white wine vinegar
2 tbsp olive oil
big pinch of salt

Combine all the ingredients in a bowl, taste for seasoning and leave to stand for 1 hour before serving.

There was once a restaurant in Gloucester Road, West London, called The Texas Lone Star. It had a wooden cigar-store Indian outside, swinging saloon doors, Rawhide on the tellies and non-stop country music. Waitresses dressed like cowgirls, the walls were plastered with antlers and Route 66 signs (they weren't sticklers for geographic accuracy), and there were pinball machines by the loos. For an eight-year-old boy, it was as close to heaven as I could imagine. What a restaurant it was, with its OK-ish Tex Mex, ten-alarm chilli and as many nachos as you could eat. It's long gone, replaced by some faceless dim sum chain, or Brazilian tea palace or whatever. But my sister's favourite dish was TLS nachos. She would just order three plates of these. Simple, covered with melted cheese, but very good indeed.

My TLS Nachos

Preheat the oven to fan 200°C/400°F/Gas 7. Cover each tortilla quarter with a big wodge of cheese. Make sure each one is separate from the next; this is not a great gooey, homogenous batch of Nachos Deluxe, rather individual bliss. Top with a jalapeño slice and bake for 5 minutes. Serve with sour cream, hot sauce and guacamole.

SERVES 6

6 corn tortillas, cut into
   quarters and fried in
   vegetable oil until crisp,
   then drained
300g/10½oz Cheddar, grated
24 pickled jalapeño slices,
   from jar

Takeaway onion bhajis are invariably drab, sullenly greasy and disappointing, having sat around for a few hours, losing any crispness and joy. But eaten fresh from the hot oil, they're wonderful street food, and a fine snack.

Onion Fritters with Cumin

SERVES 4

150g/5½oz chickpea (gram) flour
big pinch of salt
3 onions, thinly sliced
2 heaped tsp cumin seeds, toasted and ground
1 heaped tsp coriander seeds, toasted and ground
2 tbsp chopped coriander leaves
1 tsp hot chilli powder
squeeze of lemon juice
vegetable oil for deep-frying

Sift the flour into a large bowl and mix with the salt. Add the onions, cumin, coriander seeds, coriander leaves, chilli powder and lemon juice, plus 6–8 tbsp water, to make a thick batter.

In a deep, heavy pan, heat the oil to about 180°C/350°F, or until a small drop of batter sizzles fiercely, rises to the top and browns in 30 seconds. Alternatively, use an electric deep-fryer.

Drop in 1 tbsp of the batter and cook for 2–3 minutes, until golden brown. Drain and taste. If necessary, add more salt, chilli or cumin. Deep-fry the remaining fritters in batches, two or three at a time, so the oil stays hot. Let the oil heat up again after each batch. Remove with a slotted spoon and eat hot.

Classic street food from Palermo in Sicily. You want them finger-searing hot and salted with a heavy hand.

Panelle

Line a large baking sheet with baking parchment and place in the freezer for 20 minutes.

Whisk the flour into 700ml/1½ pints cold water in a pan, ensuring there are no lumps. Add the parsley and salt and cook over a lowish heat, whisking continuously, until the mixture is thick and falls away from the side of the pan. This will take about 8 minutes – beware, as it goes very thick very quickly.

Pour onto the chilled baking sheet and use a spatula or palette knife to spread it as thin as you dare. Leave to cool.

Heat the oil in a wide, deep pan to 180°C/350°F, or until a cube of bread browns in 30 seconds. Cut the mixture into tortilla chip-sized triangles and deep-fry until golden, 2–3 minutes. Drain on kitchen paper, add a squeeze of lemon juice and more salt to taste. Eat hot.

SERVES 6–8

325g/11½oz chickpea (gram)
   flour
big handful of fresh parsley,
   finely chopped
big pinch of sea salt flakes,
   plus extra to serve
sunflower oil for deep-frying
1 lemon, halved

This is the real thing, puffed and filled with lethally hot air. They're incredibly easy to make, and even better to eat, warm and stuffed with whatever takes your fancy. I got this recipe from friend and food writer Rose Prince, who learned it from Tony Kitous of Comptoir Libanais. She's not only a magnificent cook but a beautiful baker too. They are great for kebabs (see page 102) or kibbeh nayyah (see page 98).

Easy Pitta Bread

MAKES ABOUT 10

350ml/12fl oz warm water
1 tsp fast-action dried yeast
2 tbsp olive oil
600g/1lb 5oz strong white
    flour, plus extra for dusting
1 tbsp caster sugar
1 tsp salt

Pour the water into a bowl, add the yeast and stir until dissolved, then add the oil, flour, sugar and salt. Mix to make a fairly firm dough, adding more water if too dry, or more flour if too wet. Knead for 6–8 minutes, until smooth and elastic. Put in a bowl, cover and leave for 1–1½ hours, until risen.

Preheat the oven to fan 220°C/425°F/Gas 9. Divide the dough into 10 equal pieces, about 100g/3½oz each, and shape into balls. On a lightly floured surface, roll out the balls into ovals about 5mm/¼ inch thick.

Heat a baking sheet in the oven for 5 minutes. Place two or three pitta breads on the hot sheet and bake for about 4 minutes, until puffed and with a touch of colour. Place on a wire rack. Reheat the baking sheet and bake the remaining pitta breads. Serve hot.

*This requires minimal work, no kneading (well, just a few seconds' worth) or hanging about
waiting for the dough to rise. Best cooked over glowing coals, but a frying pan is fine. Serve with
curry and pickles.*

Easy Flat Bread (Roti)

MAKES 6

250g/9oz plain flour
pinch of salt
40g/1½oz cold butter, cubed
150ml/5fl oz cold water
dribble of groundnut or
**   vegetable oil**

Mix the flour and salt in a bowl, rub in the butter and make
a well in the centre, then add the water and bring together to
make a firm dough – you may need to add a drop or two more
water.

Knead for a few moments, then divide into six balls. Flatten
each ball into a thin 20cm/8-inch round, about 3mm/⅛ inch
thick.

Heat a little oil in a large, heavy-bottomed frying pan and
cook for about 1–2 minutes on each side. Or place a baking
tray on the barbecue, let it get hot, then cook the bread for
about 2–3 minutes on each side. Serve hot.

The idiosyncrasies and regional variations of American barbecue are endless. I'm not just talking about the choice of meat (beef for Texas, pork for the Carolinas and Tennessee) but also cut (rib, brisket, Boston butt, whole pig), wood variety (cherry, mesquite, apple wood) and the sauce to serve with the meat. In North Carolina there are two main sauces: vinegar-based in the east, and tomato-based in the west. And even when you've separated the state thus, there are still a million different takes on two main sauces. But both go well with pork, cutting through any fatty heft.

A Pair of North Carolina Barbecue Sauces

Vinegar-based sauce

Mix everything together in a bowl and stir until the sugar has dissolved. Store in a sterilised jar in the fridge; this will last for months.

Tomato-based sauce

Mix everything together and store in a sterilised jar in the fridge. Keeps for weeks, if not months.

VINEGAR-BASED SAUCE

MAKES 450ML/16FL OZ

450ml/16fl oz cider vinegar
1 heaped tbsp brown sugar
big pinch of salt
big pinch of freshly ground
 pepper
4–6 dried bird's-eye chillies,
 crumbled, or 1 tbsp cayenne
 pepper

TOMATO-BASED SAUCE

MAKES 350ML/12FL OZ

250ml/9fl oz cider vinegar
100ml/3½fl oz tomato ketchup
1 tsp cayenne pepper
dribble of runny honey
big pinch of salt

Clean, refreshing and crunchy, this simple salad goes with most curries, as well as with Mexican tacos. And it's great in sandwiches too.

Radish, Red Onion and Green Chilli Salad

SERVES 6 AS A SIDE DISH

1 large bunch of radishes, thinly sliced (if the leaves are on, chop and use them too)

1 red onion, finely chopped

2 green finger chillies, deseeded and finely chopped

2 tbsp white wine vinegar

big pinch of sea salt flakes

handful of fresh coriander leaves, roughly chopped

Mix all the ingredients together and leave for 20 minutes. Taste for seasoning and serve.

This is the basis of all Indonesian sambals, and is best made in big batches. It freezes well and keeps in the fridge, in an airtight jar, for up to 2 weeks. It's wonderful with eggs, in stews, and anything else that needs a kick. Make it in a well-ventilated area, or the chillies will choke you.

Sambal Ulek

MAKES 450G/1LB

450g/1lb fresh red chillies (try to avoid the Dutch ones with their insipid kick), stalks removed

1 tbsp sea salt flakes

1 tbsp white wine vinegar

2 tbsp groundnut or vegetable oil

Put the chillies in a pan and add water to cover. Bring to the boil and simmer for 20 minutes, then drain and put the chillies in a blender with the salt, vinegar and oil and blend until smooth. Store in a jar in the fridge for up to 2 weeks.

I've eaten this all over the southern USA. Sounds odd, tastes wonderful. OK, so it's a shag actually getting the rind: not difficult, but a mite labour intensive. It's good with ham or Cheddar cheese and sparks up sandwiches too.

Pickled Watermelon Rind

Cut the rind into chunks and scrape off any red flesh. Pare the hard green skin off the other side with a small, sharp knife, then cut the rind into 4–5cm/about 1½-inch cubes.

In a plastic bucket or non-metallic bowl, dissolve the salt in the water and put the rind into the salted water. Weight down the rind with a plate and leave for 24 hours. Drain and rinse well.

Mix the vinegar, sugar and spices in a large pan and simmer until the sugar has dissolved. Bring to the boil, add the lemon slices and boil for 5 minutes. Add the rind and boil for a further 2 minutes.

Put into sterilised jars and seal. Store in the fridge, and leave for at least 2 weeks before serving.

**MAKES ABOUT 1 LITRE/
1¾ PINTS**

rind from 1 large (3.5–4kg/
   8–9lb) watermelon
35g/1¼oz pickling salt or
   coarse sea salt
1 litre/1¾ pints water
1 bottle (568ml) distilled malt
   vinegar
550g/1lb 4oz white caster
   sugar
1 tbsp cloves
3 cinnamon sticks
1 star anise
2 tbsp allspice
20 black peppercorns
1 tbsp coriander seeds
1 large lemon, sliced

BASICS

There are as many variations of this spice mix as there are spluttering tuk tuks in India. And everyone has their own view as to what makes up the perfect masala. The key is use of the warming spices ('garam' means warm or hot), and the masala is usually (but not always) added at the end of cooking. The classic Mughal version uses just cardamom, cinnamon, cloves and black pepper. Nutmeg is sometimes thrown in too. It's best used with creamy, yogurt-based dishes. My version also has coriander and cumin, which makes it punchier and similar to the more widely used garam masala. Using whole spices – first roasting and grinding them – makes all the difference in the world. Store in an airtight container in a cool dark place. It will keep its potency for about two or three months.

Garam Masala

MAKES 10 TSP

1 tbsp green cardamom pods, husks cracked and seeds removed and reserved

1½ cinnamon sticks

½ tbsp cloves

1 tsp black peppercorns

1 tsp cumin seeds

1 tsp coriander seeds

Dry-roast all the ingredients in a heavy-bottomed pan over a medium heat, until you smell all those wonderful oils.

Using a mortar and pestle or a spice grinder, grind and put into an airtight container.

This gives a gentle stock, perfect for gravies and risottos. Like a young English rose, it's delicate and pale, but never insipid.

Light Chicken Stock

Put the chicken in a large pan, cover with the water, bring to the boil and skim off any scum.

Add the vegetables, herbs and peppercorns, turn down the heat so the liquid just about blip blips, and simmer, very gently, for 4 hours.

Strain through a muslin-lined sieve into a bowl and leave to cool. Store overnight in the fridge. The next morning, remove the layer of fat.

**MAKES ABOUT 3 LITRES/
5 PINTS**

3 chicken carcasses, uncooked
6 chicken wings
about 4 litres/7 pints cold
    water
1 carrot, roughly chopped
2 celery stalks, roughly
    chopped
2 tomatoes, quartered
2 white onions, quartered
a few parsley stalks
2 bay leaves
6 peppercorns

Around February, my freezer is groaning with the small bodies of deep-frozen game birds, a few the spoils of my rather second-rate shooting. Young grouse rarely make it as far as the fridge, but pheasant and partridge abound, and to be honest, by the start of February, I've had my fill of game for a few months. So I make a huge stock, which can be turned into the most fragrant, deeply flavoured broth. If you do happen to have a grouse lying about, save him for something else, as the bird tends to overpower everything. That is, unless you want to make a stock exclusively from grouse.

Game Stock

**MAKES ABOUT 3 LITRES/
5 PINTS**

**assorted game birds, such as
2 pheasant and 4 partridge,
or 1 pheasant and
5 partridge, or no pheasant
and 6 partridge. Basically,
chuck 'em all in**
2 carrots, roughly chopped
2 onions, roughly chopped
**2 celery stalks, roughly
chopped**
2 tomatoes, quartered
4 sprigs of thyme
handful of parsley stalks
6 peppercorns
1 bay leaf
2 juniper berries

Preheat the oven to fan 210°C/415°F/Gas 8. Roast the birds for about 10 minutes, then remove the meat (use for soup or a pie) and use the carcasses for the stock.

Put the carcasses in a large pan, add cold water to cover, bring to the boil and skim off any scum.

Add everything else, bring back to the boil, then turn down to the merest of simmers and simmer gently for 4 hours.

Strain through a muslin-lined sieve into a bowl.

Rather more assertive than its lily-white cousin (see page 223), this takes on the caramelised flavours of roasted bones and wings. I use it for soups and broths, as it contains the very essence of roast chicken. You can use the carcasses of old roast birds (I tend to wait until I have three in the freezer before making a batch of stock) and fresh wings, blasted, along with the vegetables, in a stinking-hot oven.

Dark Chicken Stock

MAKES ABOUT 3½ LITRES/ 6 PINTS

8 chicken wings
2 carrots, roughly chopped
3 celery stalks, roughly chopped
3 onions, quartered
3 tomatoes, quartered
olive oil
2 or 3 roast chicken carcasses (including scraps, skin, jelly)
about 4 litres/7 pints cold water
handful of coriander stalks
4 bay leaves
8 black peppercorns

Preheat the oven to fan 210°C/415°F/Gas 8. Put the wings, carrots, celery, onions and tomatoes in a roasting tin, anoint with a glug of olive oil and roast for 25 minutes, until they all have a good colour.

Put the chicken carcasses and wings in a large pan, cover with the water, bring to the boil and skim off any scum.

Add the vegetables, herbs and peppercorns, turn down the heat to a simmer and cook at a gentle 'blip, blip' for 5 hours.

Strain through a muslin-lined sieve into a bowl, leave to cool and store overnight in the fridge. Next morning, remove most of the fat. For added concentration, reduce down by half again.

Most classic cookbooks demand veal stock, and if you can get hold of veal bones from the butcher, then fine. But I tend to use beef bones, the remains from a good roast rib of beef. This stock should be rich and meaty, but not over-assertive. If you want more wobbling stock (as you do for A Summer's Tail on page 167), add a split pig's trotter. With beef, there's often a lot of fat, so do skim judiciously.

Beef Stock

Put the bones, bits and trotter in a large pan, cover with the water, bring to the boil and skim off any scum.

Add the vegetables, herbs and peppercorns, turn down the heat to a simmer and cook at a gentle 'blip, blip' for 5 hours.

Strain through a muslin-lined sieve into a bowl, leave to cool and store overnight in the fridge. Next morning, remove most of the fat. For added concentration, reduce down by half again.

MAKES ABOUT 3½ LITRES/ 6 PINTS

remains from 3 or 4 or 5 ribs
   of beef (including scraps,
   fat, jelly)
1 pig's trotter, split (optional)
about 4 litres/7 pints cold
   water
3 carrots, roughly chopped
3 celery stalks, roughly
   chopped
3 onions, quartered
3 tomatoes, quartered
handful of coriander stalks
4 bay leaves
8 black peppercorns

This is light and discreet, but still has a decent flavour. If you want more depth, fry the ingredients in a little oil for 10 or so minutes. But with this one, I'm looking for a clear, almost elusive vegetable scent.

Vegetable Stock

MAKES ABOUT 3½ LITRES/ 6 PINTS

3 onions, quartered

4 carrots, roughly chopped

3 celery stalks, roughly
   chopped

4 tomatoes, quartered

1 leek, roughly chopped

150g/5½oz mushrooms, sliced

1 head of garlic, chopped in
   half

handful of parsley stalks

2 sprigs of thyme

2 bay leaves

about 4 litres/7 pints cold
   water

Throw all the vegetables and herbs into a large pan. Cover with the water, bring to the boil, then turn down the heat and simmer for 1 hour.

Strain through a muslin-lined sieve into a bowl, making sure you press down hard on the mulch in the sieve for flavour.

SUPPLIERS

The Blackface Meat Company
www.blackface.co.uk
Lamb, mutton, beef, veal, venison, furred and feathered game.

Cool Chile Co
www.coolchile.co.uk
Many types of chillies, Mexican herbs and spice pastes, plus fresh corn tortillas and masa harina.

Ginger Pig
www.thegingerpig.co.uk
Rare-breed pork, lamb and beef.

Japanese Kitchen
www.japanesekitchen.co.uk
Mirin, sake, miso paste, kombu, bonito.

BIBLIOGRAPHY

Ayrton, Elisabeth *The Cookery of England* 1974 André Deutsch; 1977 Penguin

Boxer, Arabella *Arabella Boxer's Book of English Food* 1991 Hodder & Stoughton; 2012 Fig Tree

Burke, Virginia *Eat Caribbean* 2005 Simon & Schuster

Croft-Cooke, Rupert *English Cooking* 1960 WH Allen

David, Elizabeth *French Country Cooking* 1951 John Lehmann; 1970, 2001, 2011 Penguin

Dunlop, Fuchsia *Sichuan Cookery* 2003 Penguin. Recipe for 'Sichuan Boiled Beef' page 30 Copyright © Fuchsia Dunlop 2001. Reproduced by permission of the author c/o Rogers, Coleridge & White Ltd., 20 Powis Mews, London W11 1JN

Fielding, Henry *The Grub Street Opera*, reissued 2010 by Gale ECCO

Francesconi, Jeanne Carola *La Cucina Napoletana* 2010 Grimaldi & C.

Gordon, Victor *The English Cookbook* 1985 Jonathan Cape

Gray, Rose and Rogers, Ruth *The River Café Cook Book* 1995 Ebury Press

Guérard, Michel *Cuisine Gourmande* 1978 Macmillan

Hartley, Dorothy *Food in England* 2009 Piatkus

Lewis, Norman *Naples '44* 2002 Eland Publishing

Locatelli, Giorgio *Made in Italy: Food and Stories* 2006 Fourth Estate

MacLean, Lady Veronica *Lady Maclean's Cookbook* 1966 Collins

May, Robert *The Accomplisht Cook* 1660, most recently published by Dodo Press 2010

Norman, Russell *Polpo: A Venetian Cookbook (Of Sorts)* 2012 Bloomsbury

Olney, Richard *Simple French Food* 1974, 2003 Grub Street

Owen, Sri *Indonesian Regional Food and Cookery* 1994 Doubleday; 1999 Frances Lincoln

Parker Bowles, Tom *Let's Eat* 2012 Pavilion

Renton, Alex *Planet Carnivore: Why Cheap Meat Costs the Earth* 2013 Guardian Books (kindle)

Schwartz, Arthur *Naples at Table* 2013 William Morrow Cookbooks

Thompson, David *Thai Food* 2002 Pavilion

White, Florence *Good Things in England* 1932 Jonathan Cape; 1999 Persephone Books

Wolfert, Paula *The Cooking of South West France* 1987 Dorling Kindersley; 1999 Grub Street; 2005 John Wiley and Sons

INDEX

AUTHOR'S ACKNOWLEDGEMENTS

My mother and father, and also Laura Lopes and Ben Elliot.

Alex Bilmes, Fuchsia Dunlop, Matthew Fort, Grainne Fox, the best agent a man can have, Victor Gordon, Gerard Greaves, Geordie Greig, Miranda Harvey, Nigel Haworth, Graham Jebb, Bill Knott, Sebastian Lee, Giorgio Locatelli, Justine Pattison, Polly Powell, Maggie Ramsay, Becca Spry, Richard D Storey, David Thompson, Ewan Venters, Eunice Woolcock and Jenny Zarins.

Plus Sara, the greatest recipe tester of them all. And for putting up with me.